NOMADS of the DAWN

The Penan *of the* Borneo Rain Forest

Wade Davis • Ian Mackenzie • Shane Kennedy

Principal photography by
Ian Mackenzie and David Hiser

with additional photography by
Wade Davis, Frans Lanting, Thom Henley, Art Wolfe, and others

POMEGRANATE ARTBOOKS *San Francisco*

Published by
Pomegranate Artbooks
Box 6099, Rohnert Park, California 94927

For information concerning the Endangered Peoples Project,
please write Endangered Peoples Project, P.O. Box 1516,
Station A, Vancouver, B.C. V6C 2P7 Canada.

Photograph p. 2: Frans Lanting • Minden Pictures

Library of Congress Cataloging-in-Publication Data

Davis, Wade.
    Nomads of the dawn : the Penan of the Borneo rain forest /
Wade Davis, Ian Mackenzie, Shane Kennedy. — 1st ed.
      p.   cm.
    ISBN 0-87654-357-3 (pb)
    1. Penan (Bornean people)—Social conditions—Juvenile
literature. 2. Rain forest ecology—Malaysia—Sarawak—
Juvenile literature. 3. Sarawak—Social conditions—Juvenile
literature. I. Mackenzie, Ian. II. Kennedy, Shane. III. Title.
DS595.2.P44D36 1995
959.5'40049922—dc20   94-49449
                                     CIP

Pomegranate Catalog No. A776
Designed by Peter Howells

Printed in Korea
00 99 98 97 96 95   6 5 4 3 2 1

First Edition

CONTENTS

The authors of this book are members of the Endangered Peoples Project (EPP), a small group of scientists, photographers, writers, and filmmakers who first came together in 1989 with the goal of providing indigenous peoples with a platform from which to express their concerns directly to the world. It was the members' conviction that the demise of cultural and biological diversity was the central tragedy of our era. It was their hope that a series of books and films might draw attention to the plight of these societies and their threatened homelands, and thus contribute in some small way to a fundamental reassessment of the relationship between modern industrial society and the ancient heritage of the earth. A guiding principle of the organization was that none of the members should benefit financially from their efforts. Thus all proceeds from the sale and distribution of EPP books and films are either returned directly to the indigenous society in question or used to finance other EPP investigations. Members of the EPP receive no salaries, nor are they paid for their time and contributions. We maintain no offices and have no overhead. All contributions and grants are applied directly to the product.

Most of the materials in this book were collected during seven field trips the authors made into the interior of Sarawak. Wade Davis visited the Penan homeland in 1989 and 1993; Shane Kennedy traveled there in 1991; Ian Mackenzie in 1991 and 1992, and twice in 1993. A majority of the photographs and quotations in this book were obtained during the course of the last two trips, when Ian Mackenzie and photographer David Hiser were guests of the nomadic Penan of the Ubong River.

Nearly half the text consists of translations of statements secured in the field from Penan men, women, and children. These commentaries are a small sampling of many hours of tape recorded in the longhouses and along the endless trails of the Penan forest. That these recordings were made bears witness to the courage of the Penan, and to their willingness to take considerable risks to bring their message to the world. Since the late 1980s when they began to resist the violation of their homeland, access to the region has been sharply curtailed by the Malaysian government. Tourists may travel only in certain areas that have been carefully set aside and sanitized. Journalists are turned away. Without the active support and cooperation of the Penan, our work would not have been possible. It is they who are the real authors of this book. ❧

A NOTE ON TRANSCRIPTION

Penan belongs to the Austronesian family of languages, which includes all the languages of Borneo, as well as Malay. Like its linguistic relatives, it has a rather simple sound structure, and its pronunciation offers few difficulties to native speakers of English. In the transcription of Penan names and words, we have chosen an orthography that is both consistent and precise. Most consonants are pronounced as in English. The consonants *p*, *t*, and *k*

are unaspirated, as they are in French and Spanish. The *r* is flapped, as in Spanish and Italian. The combination *ng* is pronounced as in English, but always like "si*ng*er," never like "fi*ng*er." The apostrophe represents the glottal stop; when it directly follows a consonant, it shows that the latter is lightly glottalized. The vowels *a*, *i*, *o*, and *u* are sounded as in Spanish or Italian; *é* as in French. The letter *e*, without an accent, is the neutral vowel that one hears in the

first syllable of "*a*bout" or the last syllable of "buck*e*t." In phonetics, this sound is known as the schwa. Some vowels in Penan are long; these are written with a doubled letter, as in *Wéé*. All Penan words are very lightly stressed on the last syllable. One of the challenges an English speaker encounters with the Penan language is the fact that the schwa can be stressed. Thus the word for dart poison, *tajem*, sounds something like ta-JIM. ❦

NOMADS OF THE DAWN

ACKNOWLEDGMENTS

The creation of this book has involved many individuals in both North America and Southeast Asia. Financial assistance was generously provided by the Further Foundation, Rudy Haase and the Friends of Nature, the Western Canada Wilderness Committee, and a host of friends and supporters including Robert and Barbara Bartholomew, Frank Bonsall, William and Helen Elkins, John and Dolly Fisher, Charles B. Grace Jr., Perry and Tucker Gresh, Henry and Penelope Harris, Peter and Alice Hausmann, William and Evelyn Howard, Michael and Anne Talbot Kelly, Nicholas and Cassandra Ludington, Shelley Preston, Walter Sedgwick, Langhorne and Valerie Smith, Steven and Claire Sordoni, Hans and Susan Utsch, James and Jeanne Van Alen, William and Elizabeth Van Alen, Douglas and Lyn Walker, and Ethel B. Wister. Special thanks are due to Mr. and Mrs. William Van Alen Sr. and their grandson Alex Van Alen, who helped create many new friends for the Penan. The Endangered Peoples Project is supported by the Tides Foundation, and we would especially like to thank Penny Deleray, Denise Gums, Linda Muñoz, Drummond Pike, Chuck Savitt, and Jacqueline Schad.

In the field we were assisted by a number of kind and helpful individuals. Many of these friends live in Sarawak and for political reasons cannot be named here. They know and understand our debt of gratitude. We would also like to acknowledge others who assisted our work in various ways: Dana Attanasio, Nancy Baron, Paul Burke, Sue Currie, Anthony Dixon, Henrik Egede-Lessen, David Franzoni, Michael Talbot Kelly, Lisa Kofod, Bruno Manser, Tim Matheson, Anita Roddick, Samantha Roddick, Courtenay Valenti, Bob Weir, and Barbara Whitestone.

The actual production of the book was facilitated by many individuals. Paul George revealed through action his dedication to the Penan cause. Photographs were provided without charge by Art Wolfe, Tim Matheson, Evelyne Hong, Buah Puak, Jeff Lipmann, John Werner, and Anderson Mutang Urud. Janie Bennett of Photographers/Aspen edited and secured numerous images for the book. Research assistance was provided by Alex Van Alen, Volker Bodegom, John Kramer, and Anderson Mutang Urud. Gail Percy read and corrected the manuscript, and Peter Brosius reviewed the text for ethnographic accuracy. Candice Fuhrman represented the EPP and brought our project to Pomegranate. Many thanks are due to Thomas Burke and Allen Eddington for believing in the book, to designer Peter Howells for his elegant execution, and especially to our editor, Jill Anderson, for her excellent work and patience over these many months.

We offer very special thanks to David Hiser of Photographers/Aspen. David provided many of the most remarkable images in this book. He worked in the field under the most difficult technical conditions, and continued to shoot even after he had contracted typhus. An experience that began as a photographic assignment grew into a deep personal commitment to the Penan.

We would also like to acknowledge the pivotal role of our friend and colleague Thom Henley, one of the founders of the Endangered Peoples Project. Hearing of the plight of the nomadic Penan, he traveled to Sarawak in 1989 with a documentary film crew that included Josslyn Motha, John Werner, and Paul Giacomantonio. During their time in the forest, they met a remarkable young Penan man named Dawat Lupung and recorded a lengthy interview with him. Upon his return to Canada, Thom met with Paul George and Adriane Carr of the Western Canada Wilderness Committee, who offered to publish a book based on Dawat Lupung's testimony. In the fall of 1989 Henley returned to Sarawak and was joined there by Wade Davis. This marked the beginning of a collaboration that led to *Penan: Voice for the Borneo Rainforest,* a book published in Canada in the late summer of 1990. In the fall of that year Henley led an international tour that enabled three indigenous leaders from Sarawak to bring their message to eighteen nations on three continents. It was because of Thom that the three of us became involved both with the Penan campaign and with the EPP. Without his inspiration, this book would never have come about.

Naturally, our greatest debt is to the Penan themselves. To the people of Long Iman, Long Sabai, Batu Bungan, Long Bangan, Long Latei, Long Napir, Long Keremeu, and Long Kerong, we offer our most sincere gratitude. A special thanks is owed to the people of the Ubong River, whose photos and interviews form the heart of this book. Finally, we would like to acknowledge all the individuals and organizations around the world working to defend the homeland of the indigenous peoples of Sarawak. Of all these remarkable activists, one young man stands out. Anderson Mutang Urud, a Kelabit from Long Napir, worked for many years in Sarawak before being forced into exile by the Malaysian authorities. Mutang has become our friend and colleague, a source of inspiration and a constant reminder of the meaning of sacrifice. His struggle continues, and it is to Andy that we dedicate this book. ❧

They walked into my office one winter day, looking a little like visitors from another millennium, their straw headgear and wooden bracelets the only remnants of the culture they had left behind, wearing borrowed sweaters as protection against the unaccustomed cold. Using a translator who had painstakingly learned their language, the Penan described how the logging companies had set up floodlights to continue their destruction of the forest all through the night as well as the day. Like the shell-shocked inhabitants of a city under siege, they described how not even the monsoon rains slowed the chain saws and logging machinery that were destroying the ancestral home of their people.

These are the front lines of the war against nature now raging throughout the world. The weak and the powerless are the early victims, but the relentless and insatiable drive to exploit and plunder the earth will soon awaken the conscience of others who are only now beginning to interpret the alarms and muffled cries for help.

VICE PRESIDENT AL GORE
from *Earth in the Balance*

The people of the so-called developed world have always treated tribal people as total savages, be it to enslave them, subdue them, civilize them, or convert them to our way of thinking. Even now, as the Penan of Sarawak are harassed and even imprisoned for defending their tribal rights . . . even now, the dreadful pattern of collective cultural genocide continues.

H.R.H. THE PRINCE OF WALES
From a speech delivered at the Royal Botanic Garden—Kew
As reported in *The Daily Telegraph*
February 7, 1990

Sometimes civilization is forced upon us.

MAHATHIR MOHAMAD
Prime Minister of Malaysia
Speaking at an ASEAN conference
Singapore, October 4, 1992

Asik Nyelit, headman, Ubong River band.

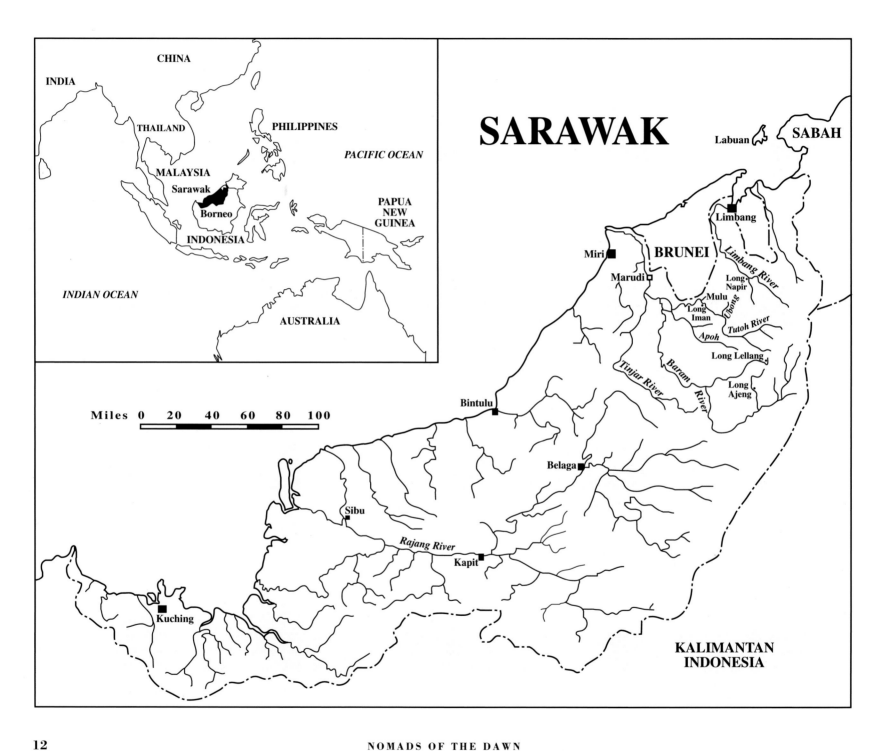

SARAWAK

CHINA

INDIA

THAILAND
PHILIPPINES

PACIFIC OCEAN

MALAYSIA

Sarawak

Borneo

INDONESIA

INDIAN OCEAN

PAPUA
NEW
GUINEA

AUSTRALIA

Labuan
SABAH

Limbang

Miri
BRUNEI

Marudi

Long
Napir

Mulu

Long
Iman

Apoh

Long Lellang

Long
Ajeng

Tinjar River

Baram River

Tutoh River

Ubong

Limbang River

Miles 0 20 40 60 80 100

Bintulu

Belaga

Sibu

Rajang River

Kapit

Kuching

KALIMANTAN
INDONESIA

THOM HENLEY

Dawat Lupung.

ART WOLFE

Tu'o Pejuman, headman,
Long Iman.

For over a million years all human beings were nomads, wanderers on a pristine earth. Our Paleolithic ancestors believed in the power of the animals, accepted the existence of magic, acknowledged the potency of the spirit. Magical and mystical ideas entered the very texture of their thinking.

A mere ten thousand years ago the Neolithic revolution and the development of agriculture changed forever the relationship between humans and the earth. The agrarian transformation and the advent of sedentary village life, which led in turn to the first religious hierarchies, meant the death of ancient animistic traditions. As the cult of the seed overthrew the hunt, so the priest displaced the shaman. With religious leaders serving as mere functionaries of established religious theologies, the shaman's poetry, inspired by the songs of ten thousand birds, was turned into prose.

A new theme entered history. The separation between humanity and nature set in motion a savage assault upon the earth by human societies that in time came to pride themselves on their aversion to all forms of myth, magic, and mysticism, cultures that grew to view intimacy with nature as a poetic conceit.

The consequences of this worldview lie all around us. We have contaminated the air, water, and soil; driven wild things to extinction; dammed the rivers; torn down the ancient forests; poisoned the rain; and ripped holes in the heavens.

Who can doubt that we must dream new dreams, find new topographies of the spirit, rediscover the scents and sounds and possibilities of an earth fresh with the promise of life and wisdom? The Penan of northern Borneo by their example give us a sense of what we all once were. In their memories lie the origin and essence of the entire human race. ❦

MEMORIES AND ORIGINS

The mouth of the Baram River is the color of the earth. To the north, the soils of Sarawak disappear into the South China Sea and fleets of empty Japanese freighters hang on the horizon, awaiting the tides and a chance to fill their holds with raw logs ripped from the forests of Borneo. The river settlements are settings of opportunity and despair— muddy logging camps and clusters of shanties, their leprous facades patched with sheets of metal, plastic, and scavenged boards. Children by the river's edge dump barrels of garbage, which drifts back to shore in the wake of each passing log barge. For miles the river is choked with debris and silt, and along its banks lie thousands of logs stacked thirty deep, some awaiting shipment, some slowly rotting in the tropical heat.

A hundred miles upriver is another world, a varied and magical landscape of forest and soaring mountains, dissected by crystalline rivers and impregnated by the world's most extensive network of caves and underground passages. This is the homeland of the Penan, one of the few remaining nomadic peoples of the rain forest. Related in spirit to the Mbuti pygmies of Zaire and the wandering Makú of the northwest Amazon, the Penan draw their life from the land, moving as hunters and gatherers through the immense and remote forested uplands that give rise to the myriad affluents of the Baram and Limbang Rivers of northern Borneo. ❦

IAN MACKENZIE

Menteri and Lia, two boys raised among the Ubong River Penan, one of the last nomadic bands living within Borneo's rain forest.

Now all my contemporaries are dead, and I am the only one of them who is still here today to tell you of what life was like in the past. If you want to know the story of our origins here, I can tell you everything. Everything I say is the truth. I do not lie. I will not deceive you. I am not boasting. Everything I tell you is true. My name is Wéé Salau. There is no one older than myself. There is no one else who knows the things that I know. And now you will know about our life here. This is the suffering and hardship that we are now living with.

This is the place of our origins. This is our home, this land of the Ubong River, of the Magoh River. It is as if this land were our longhouse. This is the land of our origins. I tell the children that this is our land, that this is our longhouse, this Ubong River, this Magoh River. We have never moved, we have never left this land.

I come from no place but here. That is why I stay here. I was born right here, just up the hill, up the river. That's how long I've been roaming this area. I can never get lost in this area. This is where I was born. Ever since I was a tiny child, and my parents carried me, and led me by the hand, I have lived here. Ever since I was a little child, ever since I became an adult, I have remained here, on the Ubong River. Just as the longhouse people have their place, we, too, have ours; even though we do not live in a longhouse, this is our place, this area along the Ubong River, where we wander. My mother and father never wanted to move from this land. Surely we never went to any other place, we remained here, in the land of the rivers, in our land. At this Ubong River, and also the Magoh River, this is where my parents brought me up; on the left side, and on the right side, we lived along the Magoh River. Truly it is so, at the confluence of those streams upriver, on the left side and on the right side, that is the place where we lived. We could never get lost, for we are so familiar with this country. This is truly our land.

After I grew up, after I married and had children, I wandered the length and breadth of our territory. I have been everywhere in the land of the Ubong and the Magoh Rivers. At the Puak River, at the Barei, these are the places I have lived. At the Seladih, over on that side, that is where we lived. At the River Tepen near here, that is where we lived. At the big river, that is where we lived. My wife from before, my first wife, she died, and then I married again and had more children. I have never moved away from this land.

We have stayed here and hunted boar, and hunted birds, and hunted deer, and obtained our food. Certainly we have never left this land. My grandfather and my grandmother and my mother and my father are all dead, but they died here, they didn't die in any other place. They died here, at the Ubong River, at the Magoh River, and the old headman, the headman before me, he died here, right at this very spot, at Bila Creek. At the Sepugung River, at the Malai River, at the Tepen River, at the Ya'ong River. And the headman Tamen Tering, and old Lawai, this is the place where they died. This is where we have always lived, this is where we have always stayed.

WÉÉ SALAU
the elder headman,
Ubong River band
April 1993

Wéé Salau, the late headman of the Ubong River Penan. Though his age was uncertain, at the time of his death in 1994 he was doubtless one of the oldest nomads in Asia. For the last years of his life he was unable to walk, and was carried from encampment to encampment as his people moved through the forest.

Memories and Origins

It is just after dawn and the sound of gibbons runs across the canopy of the forest. In the valley far below the smoke of cooking fires mingles with the mist. A hunting party returns, and even from this height one can tell by the movement of the men that they have killed a wild boar. One shot and the people eat for a week. From this mountaintop where generations of Penan have come to pray, one looks out over a pristine rain forest, past the clear headwaters of one of Sarawak's ancient rivers to the distant mountains that rise toward the heart of Borneo. There on the horizon, coming over the mountains from seven directions and descending into the valley to precisely the same elevation, are the scars of advancing logging roads. The nearest is but three miles from this encampment of nomadic Penan. When the wind is right, the sound of chain saws may be heard, even in the middle of the night. There is today virtually nowhere in Penan territory free of the sound of machinery. If the Sarawak government continues to have its way, this valley will very soon be laid waste, and the people will be forced from the land. ❧

 And in the old days a headman, at this place on the river, was contacted by the British; this was the beginning of the time when we were governed by the British, and I can remember it. When the British came here in the old days, certainly this was our place. In the old days when there were no airplanes, and there were no bulldozers, and one walked everywhere, for there were no roads, there were no trucks.

WÉÉ SALAU
Ubong River
April 1993

Memories and Origins

We yearn for the sounds of the forest. We have always heard these sounds. In the time of our grandparents long ago we heard these sounds. That is why we still yearn to hear them. In those times long ago, our lives were satisfying, our lives were fulfilled. And now it is harder for us, because we hear the sound of bulldozers. And that is what we always talk about, we women, when we get together. How will we live, how will we thrive, now that we have all these new problems? To us the sound of bulldozers is the sound of death. We feel sorrowful, we weep, when we see the forest that has been destroyed, when we see the red land. *Tusa na'an' tana' bala, kebit kebit urip jin sahau, b'é' pun tana' bala, b'é' pun tusa.* It is hard for us to look at the red land.

LEJENG KUSIN
Ubong River
May 1993

Lejeng Kusin.

WADE DAVIS

The Penan homeland, as seen from the flank of Gunung Api.

In the time of our fathers the tropical rain forests stood immense, inviolable, a mantle of green stretching across entire continents. That era is no more. Today in many parts of the tropics the clouds are made of smoke, the scent is of grease and lube oil, and the sounds one hears are of machinery, the buzz of chain saws, and the cacophony of enormous reptilian earth movers hissing and moaning with exertion. It is a violent overture, like the opening notes of an opera about war, a war between humans and the land, a wrenching terminal struggle to make the latter conform to the whims and designs of the former. The residue of this conflict now colors the landscape of Sumatra and Brazil, Zaire and Madagascar, Gabon and Cameroon, and a hundred other lands once covered by tropical rain forests.

The rain forests of Southeast Asia are particularly imperiled. The primary forests that once blanketed much of Thailand and the Philippines no longer exist. The demise of the rain forests of Burma, Indonesia, and Papua New Guinea is imminent. While Brazil accounts for only 2.4 percent of world tropical timber exports, Malaysia is responsible for nearly half, with most of the wood coming from the East Malaysian states of Sabah and Sarawak. Sabah is expected to be logged out soon, and has been forced to curtail the export of whole logs. In Sarawak the export of unprocessed timber increased from 6.7 million cubic meters in 1980 to 18.8 million in 1990. The World Bank reports that trees are being harvested at four times the sustainable rate. The rate of cut in

Sarawak is, in fact, among the highest the world has ever known. If current forestry policies continue, within five to seven years all of Sarawak's original forest outside of a few protected parks will be gone.

As the forests fall, the indigenous cultures suffer the most, the very people who over the course of thousands of years have developed an intimate knowledge of the land, men and women who, lacking the technology to transform the forest, chose instead long ago to understand it. Now, with hundreds of tribal groups facing assimilation or destruction, we stand to lose in a single generation the accumulated wisdom of millennia. 🌿

Kalang.

The mythologies of most indigenous peoples of Borneo speak of ancient migrations from other parts of Southeast Asia. The Penan, as Wéé Salau tells us, believe they live in the land of their origins. According to one of their stories, the first man and woman were alone and knew nothing of reproduction and birth. There was a tree deep in the forest that had a wide hole in its trunk, just above the ground. Nearby was another tree with a large branch that pointed to the cavity in the first tree. One day a storm blew, and the man and woman watched as the two trees twisted in the wind, until suddenly the branched tree fell onto the other, penetrating the cavity again and again as the wind buffeted the forest. Man and woman came together, imitating the trees, and thus were conceived the children that gave rise to the Penan. ✿

 This is a story from long, long ago, which the elders have told me. Once there were two brothers, and their mother gave birth to a child. After the birth of the child, the mother gave the two brothers the placenta to eat. And after the two brothers had eaten it, and realized what it was, they got angry. So then they ran away from the village. They ran away because they were angry. And when they were far away from the village, they started to talk, to make a deal. There was a stream in front of them, and they agreed to jump across it. Whichever one should land on the other side would become a tiger, and whichever one should fall into the water would become a crocodile. So first one, and then the other, leapt off the bank. One landed on the other side, and the other fell into the stream. Then they spoke to each other: "We are separate now; one of us will be of the land, and the other will be of the river. And we may not attack people for no reason. Only if they do something wrong can we attack and kill them." So that is the story. The crocodile and the tiger are good brothers. And that is why the Penan people cannot kill them, for both the crocodile and the tiger are Penan people. In the forest we cannot kill the tiger. Only if the tiger does something wrong to us can we kill it. It is the same for crocodiles. Only if a crocodile does something wrong can you kill him. But if he does no wrong, then you cannot kill him. And if you do something wrong, then he can kill you. That is what we believe.

JOKIM
a young man
Long Sabai
February 1993

Born of the forest and dependent on it for every aspect of their material lives, the Penan long ago embarked on a journey that knew no end. Fearful of the heat of the sun, ignorant of the seas, insulated from the heavens by the branches of the canopy, their entire cognitive and spiritual world became based on the forest. Distance and time became measured not in hours or miles but rather in the quality of the experience itself. With good hunting a trip is short, though it might be measured by a Westerner in weeks. A long, arduous walk is one that exposes the Penan to the sun. The length of a journey is determined in the moment, by the discovery of wild fruits, a stand of sago, the chance to kill a wild boar. The passage of time is measured by the activities of insects, the sweat bees that emerge two hours before dusk, the black cicadas that electrify the forest at precisely six in the evening. If there is a pattern to the Penan migration, it is determined by the growth cycle of the sago palm. It is a journey that may take twenty years to complete, an itinerary first described by the ancestors at a time when the earth was young and still wet with the innocence of birth. ❧

 We are fortunate, like a bird who has wings. We can fly to anywhere we please. If the place where we have built our houses becomes dirty, or muddy, or slippery, and not good anymore, we just move away. If we want to go far away, we move to a place that is far; if we want to live nearby, we move to a place nearby. This is the way it has always been. When we are walking, and we feel like stopping, we might stay in one place for just one or two days, or three days. And if we want to move, we just move, we move to any place that we choose.

Thus it has been since our origins, for us Penan who live in the forest. We always move, and always look for a place that we like, a place where we can be happy. And we look for an area where there are many animals, where the sago is plentiful. And we look for a place where the river is near, and where the water is good, where it is easy to make good sago. That is where we stay. That is why we are always moving.

LEJENG KUSIN
Ubong River
May 1993

*Nomadic Penan never build
their shelters on the shores of
rivers. Several times a day,
women and children carry
water in bamboo tubes to
their ridgetop encampments.*

Straddling the equator and stretching eight hundred miles east to west and six hundred miles north to south, Borneo is the third-largest island on earth. Six major rivers and literally hundreds of smaller streams drain the isolated center of the island where the mountains of Kalimantan rise to almost ten thousand feet. Politically the island is claimed by three nations. Indonesian Kalimantan encompasses the southern two-thirds, while to the north the small, oil-rich sultanate of Brunei is flanked by the Malaysian states of Sarawak and Sabah.

Sarawak joined the Federation of Malaysia in 1963. Before that, it had been under the direct or indirect influence of the English for over a hundred years. In 1841, a British adventurer named James Brooke, supported by the ships of the Royal Navy, established what became a virtual trading monopoly in Sarawak and laid the foundations of a remarkable family dynasty. Known as the White Rajahs of Sarawak, the male scions of the Brooke family ruled until 1946 when, in the twilight of the British Empire, Vyner Brooke ceded control of Sarawak to Britain. The terms under which Sarawak joined the Malaysian Federation in 1963 were precise and historically significant. All matters of defense, security, taxation, and control of the vast petroleum reserves were placed under the authority of the federal government in Kuala Lumpur. The state government of Sarawak, however, retained complete control of forest resources, and of all matters related to land tenure and utilization.

Today, Malaysia is a country of fifteen million, a net producer of oil and the world's leading exporter of tin, palm oil, rubber, pepper, and tropical timber. Sarawak encompasses roughly 38 percent of Malaysian territory and has a population of approximately 1.6 million. Within this state are some twenty-seven distinct ethnic groups. The Islamic Melanau and Malay comprise one-fifth of the population. Thirty percent are Chinese or recent immigrants from throughout Southeast Asia. Close to half the population, however, is native, representing more than a dozen cultures including the Iban, Bidayuh, Kenyah, Kayan, Kedayan, Murut, Punan, Bisayah, Kelabit, Berawan, and Penan. Today, these indigenous peoples are known collectively as *Dayaks*, a generic term that dates only to the time of the British.

Most of these peoples are sedentary farmers who dwell in communal longhouses and have long practiced shifting rice cultivation. The traditionally nomadic Penan fall into two major groups, distinguished by differences of dialect and culture. The Western Penan, numbering today some 2,200, are centered in the Belaga district and the Silat River. The more numerous Eastern Penan, some 4,300 strong, live in the Baram River basin. As recently as 1960, the vast majority of all Penan were nomadic. The last of the nomadic Western Penan settled in 1970. Of the thousands of indigenous peoples who roamed the forests of Borneo at the turn of this century, only eight bands of Eastern Penan remain fully nomadic. These comprise approximately 360 individuals, among them the people photographed in this book. Globally they represent one of the very few extant societies of wanderers. ❧

The Pinnacles of Gunung Mulu were carved by wind and water from the limestone formations that underlie much of the Penan homeland.

Eighty percent of Borneo is blanketed by extraordinarily rich tropical rain forests, part of what many believe to be the oldest and richest terrestrial ecosystem on earth. The forests of Southeast Asia originated long before the extinction of the dinosaurs and have flourished continuously for approximately 180 million years. During the Pleistocene glaciations, when global climate change transformed much of the equatorial African and Amazonian rain forest to dry land savanna, Southeast Asia's rain forests, surrounded by water, retained their moist climatic regime. Millions of years of evolution, uninterrupted by major climatic transformations, has resulted in what may be the most diverse and complex forest on earth.

The island of Borneo rose from the sea only fifteen million years ago, and during the Pleistocene, when sea levels dropped as polar ice caps expanded, a land bridge formed to the mainland of Southeast Asia. As a result Borneo was colonized by the ancient forests. Since that distant era, the climate and geology of the island have remained remarkably stable, and this, together with a lack of volcanic activity or typhoons, has left the forests relatively undisturbed for millennia. Until this century, human impact was slight, largely limited to the shifting fields of swidden agriculturalists who dwelt on the coast and in the broad river valleys of the interior. The forested hinterland remained, until now, largely unscathed.

 Whenever we feel tired, we feel strong again when we look at our beautiful forest, the forest that is so pleasant. And when we are in the forest and hear the sounds, like the hornbill, the monkeys, and the other animals, when we hear them eating fruit, these sounds make us so happy. When we hear these sounds, we feel deeply content, like the feeling you have after eating a good meal, and we feel proud, too. The sound of birds, the sound of the *merak* bird that lives in the forest, these sounds make us feel happy and fulfilled. And when we see an *uvud* sago palm, or a *jaka* sago palm, the mere sight of it makes us feel as happy as if we had already eaten it, because we are so content just looking at all the things in the forest that belong to us. And we are reminded of days gone by, of our grandparents who are dead now, when we look at all the things in the forest; we are reminded of them, too, and this comforts us, and we feel satisfied and content.

LEJENG KUSIN
Ubong River
May 1993

The flying dragon of Borneo is an arboreal lizard the size of a rat.
Membranes of skin attached to elongated ribs enable it to glide.

For the Penan the rain forest is alive, pulsing, responsive in a thousand ways to their physical needs and their spiritual readiness. Its products include roots that cleanse, leaves that cure, edible fruits and seeds, and magical plants that empower hunting dogs and dispel the forces of darkness. There is a liana that smolders for days and allows for the transport of fire. There are plants that yield glue to trap birds, toxic latex for poison darts, rare resins and gums for trade, twine for baskets, leaves for shelter and sandpaper, wood to make blowpipes, boats, tools, and musical instruments. For the Penan all of these plants are sacred, possessed by souls and born of the same earth that gave birth to the people.

Identifying both psychologically and cosmologically with the rain forest and depending on it for all their diet and technology, it is not surprising that the Penan are exceptionally skilled naturalists. It is the sophistication of their interpretation of biological relationships that is astounding. Not only do they recognize such conceptually complex phenomena as pollination and dispersal, they understand and accurately predict animal behavior. They anticipate flowering and fruiting cycles of all edible forest plants, know the preferred foods of most forest animals, and may even explain where any animal prefers to pass the night.

This knowledge of the forest, impressive as it is, speaks little of the spirit of the people. This one must sense in quiet moments, in gesture and repartee, and in dozens of representative actions that become symbols of the space through which these people live and die. To witness a headman distributing a gift of tobacco, the grace with which a hunter stalks his prey, the patience of children who know in the fiber of their being that all the gifts of the forest are to be shared—these moments tell you something of what it means to be Penan. 🌿

Kurau Kusin, headman,
Long Kidah.

DAVID HISER / PHOTOGRAPHERS / ASPEN

Every forest sound, for the Penan, is an element of a language of the spirit. Trees bloom when they hear the lovely song of the bare-throated *kankaput.* Bird calls heard from a certain direction bear good tidings; the same sounds heard from a different direction may be a harbinger of ill. Entire hunting parties may be turned back by the call of a banded kingfisher, the cry of a bat hawk. Other birds, like the spiderhunter, summon the Penan to the kill. Before embarking on a long journey, they must see a white-headed hawk flying from right to left, they must hear the call of the crested rain bird and the doglike sound of the barking deer.

To be in the forest is to experience both well-being and danger. There are malevolent spirits of land and water, venomous snakes and sun bears, wild boar whose formidable tusks can tear a man open in moments. By far the greatest peril is the wind. *Bale' Liwen* is the spirit of thunder, a male personage who lives in the sky. When he unleashes the storms that rage over the canopy, the Penan often huddle beneath their shelters, senses alert for the sound of snapping roots that may presage the collapse of a forest tree. For fear of falling branches, which through time have accounted for many deaths, the Penan never camp close to the largest trees. ❦

At the time of our origins, there was a *lamin*, a shelter, like the one that people are sleeping in here. There was a man who went out hunting, and on his return he caught a python. This man had a wife, and he told the wife, "Please do not eat this snake." Then he went off hunting again, and when he was gone, she cooked it, and it was very tasty. "No wonder my husband didn't want me to eat it, because it was so tasty"—that was the thought in her heart. Because her husband did not return, she ate some more pieces. Then she felt itchy all over, and began to scratch. She looked down and saw the pattern of the python on her skin. The more itchy she was, the more she scratched, and soon she was transformed completely into a *penganen*.

When her husband returned from the forest, he was greeted by a snake shaking its tail, but the snake still had the head of a Penan. "That was the reason I told you not to eat the python," her husband said, "because I knew you'd turn into a python." Then the wife said, "I certainly cannot remain with you anymore, so carry me to a pool in the stream." So the husband took her to a big pool. Until then the snake's head was still the wife's head. She said, "If you hear a loud noise, that is the moment when my head will be transformed, so do not look back." As he was walking away, he heard a great noise from the water, and so he didn't look back. Then that python turned into a water dragon. That water dragon is a Penan. That is how we get magical power from the waterfall.

TU'O PEJUMAN
headman, Long Iman
February 1993

Rémen Paren and his family on the trail to Batu Bungan. Virtually everything they own is carried on their backs.

opposite:
Ukun Kusin preparing thatch.

And whether we take the path along the river, or take the path beneath the trees, or take the path through the forest, we feel successful and fulfilled, for we are taking the same path as our ancestors. When we are moving, we don't walk fast. We walk slowly and take it easy. Whenever we want to sit and rest, we sit and rest. Whenever we want to stop, we just stop. That is how we manage, when we are moving and carrying big loads. We walk as slowly as we please. *Lakau posot, lakau menyun.* We walk and we stop, we walk and we sit down. *Lakau kep'éh, lakau menyun.* Then we walk on again, then we sit down again. When our load feels too heavy, we put it down; when we feel rested and strong again, we walk on. If we are moving and are carrying heavy things on our backs, and we reach a river, if we feel hot, we go down to it and bathe. We all bathe, adults and children, we bathe whenever we want. We never have it very hard when we are traveling. People sometimes say that life for us in the forest is hard, but in fact it's not hard at all.

And when we arrive at the place where we want to build our house, at the place that is good, that is suitable, there is no really hard work. All we have to do is find a few palm fronds for the roof, cut a few saplings, and build our house. That's all we have to do. When we arrive there, even the smallest child does his share. Each person finds wood or does whatever he has to do. All of us work together, cutting saplings, building the house, making the floor. So when we arrive there, the father works on the construction, the children fetch saplings and cut firewood, and the mother digs up earth to make the hearth. And we feel truly successful, and we know that our life is happy, when we find a good site to build our house, a site that we really like. A place that is cool, that has good air. Here our life is good, and we are happy, because the wind is fresh and our place is beautiful.

LEJENG KUSIN
Ubong River
May 1993

IAN MACKENZIE

A shelter can be built in four hours, and may be occupied for several days or several weeks.

So these are our houses, our houses that are made of trees; and even though the posts that support them are slender, no thicker than my arm here, ever since former times, from the time of the British, we have bound them together using thin rattan, rattan *sepa'*. And our houses are built from rattan, from wooden poles, from leaves, and are not built like the houses in town, where they use nails and zinc and cement, while we use leaves and rattan, and we have built our houses like this from the time of the British up to the present. We have built our houses like this from the time of the British up to the present, this is how we live; and some of us die, there are some of us who think we will die because this forest is being destroyed. And if this forest is not destroyed, then we can live, even though our houses are small, and bound together with rattan.

ASIK NYELIT
headman,
Ubong River band
May 1993

The fire is built on a thin pad of red clay. Once the family moves on, and the forest reclaims the site, the only evidence of former habitation will be the small pit from which the soil of the hearth was dug.

Like most hunting and gathering peoples, the Penan are egalitarian and nonhierarchical. The headman in each band acts as a spokesperson but wields no power. The position is not hereditary, and the title may sometimes be shared by two individuals. The social structure is based on an extended network of obligations mediated by a host of kin ties and a complex naming system that links the generations even as it aligns the living with the dead. Penan do not have family names. A child, boy or girl, takes as a second name that of the father, and retains it through marriage and until death.

In the absence of social stratification there are few specialists. Although certain individuals may be more talented than others at specific tasks—most notably the blowpipe maker, whose craft is highly skilled and mastered by few—the nomadic adaptation demands self-sufficiency; each person must be capable of participating in the societal activities appropriate to his or her gender.

Asik Nyelit and his son Menteri Asik. The Penan have no word for "intelligent"; their equivalent term translates as "clever at talking." Asik, because of his eloquence, was chosen by the Ubong River band as their headman. At the time this photograph was taken, Wéé Salau, who was immobilized by arthritis, was recognized as the elder headman. Asik was the headman "for walking."

IAN MACKENZIE

Ukun Kusin plays the pagang, *a musical instrument fashioned from a segment of bamboo. Only women may play the* pagang. *Should a man try, he will run the risk of being mauled by a bear on his next hunting foray.*

In general, the women's sphere is the encampment. Much of their day is taken up with raising children, preparing food, gathering wood and water, and weaving rattan into baskets and mats. Although they participate in the preparation of sago, women never hunt, and they seldom travel far in the forest unless accompanied by men or boys. Most foraging is done by men, who depart each morning, alone or in small groups, to obtain meat or fish, fell sago, or gather various products of the forest—latex for poison darts, wood for blowpipes, beeswax for torches, and various trade items such as rattan and precious resins. Whatever the activity, adult Penan usually are accompanied by children, for all knowledge is acquired through experience.

Proper behavior is learned by example rather than through rigorous discipline. In Penan culture there are no sharp distinctions between play, work, and education. The importance of sharing is instilled in children from the earliest age.

Laki Ayau playing the keringon', *or nose flute.*

Young boys mastering the use of a blowpipe, for example, are encouraged to divide even the smallest of prey, allotting equal portions of the meat to other children. In one instance, a young Penan who had gone hungry for several days killed a *teléé,* a pygmy squirrel, which he cooked and consumed alone. His failure to apportion the meat provoked not anger but laughter on the part of the adults. They simply bestowed on the boy the name *Teléé,* so that he would never forget his deed.

Perhaps the greatest transgression in Penan society is *sihun,* a term that translates roughly as a failure to share. Dependent on the forest for life, and on each other for survival, the Penan have, in effect, institutionalized individual generosity as a means of insulating the group as a whole from the uncertainties inherent in a hunting and gathering way of life. Virtually all outside observers have commented on the lack of apparent conflict within traditional Penan society. Violent arguments and physical abuse are almost unknown. The Penan themselves acknowledge this cultural trait, and express surprise and disapproval when violent interactions occur among themselves or with members of neighboring communities. So rare is physical confrontation that a single incident can be memorialized for all time. For example, in the territory of the Western Penan is a house site where, some forty years ago, two women quarreled furiously over an accusation of adultery. This locality is now known as *Lamin Pagem,* "the house of hair pulling." ❧

DAVID HISER • PHOTOGRAPHERS / ASPEN

44   NOMADS OF THE DAWN

When I had hunted enough animals, when I had good relationships with people, only then could I think of taking a wife. If I had only thought of finding a wife, but did not mix well with people or had not hunted enough animals, then she would not have wanted me. So that's how it is. If a woman sees that you can hunt, only then does she want you. After I had brought back many *babui* [wild boar] and other animals, after I had traveled and met many people, after I had learned to find sago, only then did I go and touch her hand. Only then did I go and touch her hand. She gave me a bracelet and I made her a sago fork. Only then did I ask her, "Do you have a true heart?" And she said, "As for me, if I die, I will die with you. I will always stay with you. I will not run here and there." Then I told her, "I also will die. And even if there are many women, I will not take one here, take one there. I will be faithful to you alone. I will die in your arms." This is the way we talked. Then our parents asked if we were sure of our feelings. If it was best that our hearts be united. Then they said, "The husband must never mistreat his wife and the wife must never mistreat her husband. You must live together in harmony. If the husband gets sick, the wife must take care of him. If the wife gets sick, the husband must take care of her." So that is how the elders advised us. That is how we became united. To keep the parents happy we lived with them for some time. Only when we were close to having a baby did we make our own house.

ASIK NYELIT
Tutoh River
February 1993

 My people have lived in Ubong River since the days of Tamen Tering, who later was succeeded by Tamen Lajé, who was succeeded by Paren Kusin, who was succeeded by Dulit Lesu, who was succeeded by me. There were other headmen before Tamen Tering, but now they are gone.

Ubong River is our home. Our ancestors chose this place as their home. They were born and they have lived, died, and were buried here. They also told us where the sago palms were found. They showed us where to look for the fruit trees. They have asked us to look after the land and to take care of the palms and fruits so that future generations have land to live in and food to survive on. And, likewise, I have told my children the same thing. Even now, you can ask my children; they can tell you where to find all the palm and fruit trees.

ASIK NYELIT
Marudi
December 1988

Trees sustain life in all its myriad forms—from the hornbill nesting in the hollow of a trunk to the tiny frogs swimming in the catchment of an epiphytic plant suspended a hundred feet above the forest floor. A source of warmth and food, medicine and poison, trees create the air that creatures breathe, the clouds that envelop the sun, the shelter that protects the living from a violently blue sky. For the Penan, trees represent life itself. For them, the notion of measuring a tree by the value of its raw lumber is incomprehensible. "From the forest," they say, "we get our life."

As anthropologist Peter Brosius suggests, the Penan view the forest as a homeland, an intricate, living network of economically and culturally significant places linking past, present, and future generations. Imposed from their imagination and experience is a geography of the spirit that delineates time-honored territories and ancient routes that resonate with the place names of rivers and mountains, caves, boulders, and trees. For streams alone, the Penan have over two thousand names, each imbued with its own history and legend. Some are named for a particular plant or geographic feature. Others recall events, a death or birth, the site of a raid. One river in the land of the Western Penan is known as *Be Mengen Akem Japi*. Many years ago a man named Akem Japi returned to its headwaters to find his daughter dead. In his grief he was embraced by the other Penan who lived there. Thus the stream is named, "the river at which Akem Japi was held."

When Asik Nyelit says "Our ancestors chose this place as their home," he, like all Penan, recognizes that he walks literally in the footsteps of his predecessors and that his descendants will one day follow in his. A sense of stewardship permeates Penan culture, dictating consistently the manner in which the people utilize and share their environment. Among the Western Penan the notion of stewardship is encapsulated in *molong*, a concept that defines both a conservation ethic and a notion of resource ownership. To *molong* a sago palm is to harvest the trunk with care, ensuring that the tree will sucker up from the roots. *Molong* is climbing a fruiting tree rather than cutting it down, harvesting only the largest fronds of the rattan, leaving the smaller shoots of bamboo that they may reach proper size in another year. Whenever the Penan *molong* a fruit tree, they place an identifying sign on it, a wooden marker or a cut of a machete. It is a notice of effective ownership and a public statement that the natural product is to be preserved for harvesting at a later time. In this way, through time, the Western Penan have allocated specific resources—a clump of sago, fruit trees, dart poison trees, rattan stands, fishing sites, medicinal plants—to individual kin groups. The Penan acknowledge these as familial rights that pass down through the generations.

The material culture of the Penan, like that of all nomadic peoples, is by necessity rudimentary; what few objects they keep must satisfy all of their basic needs. Their technology, therefore, is simple but elegant, and predictably based on the continual harvesting of forest plants. One of the most important resources is rattan, which provides the raw material for baskets, mats, wrist and ankle bracelets, roofing, and general tying. The Penan regularly gather at least twenty-five different species in three genera of rattan palms. The most important is *Calamus,* a genus of climbers with leaflets modified as spiny hooks that act as grapples, allowing the plant to grow up from the forest floor as it spreads as much as five hundred feet through the canopy of the rain forest.

With rattan, Penan women weave intricate and beautifully patterned artifacts that are renowned among the neighboring Dayaks. These woven objects include baskets of many sizes, backpacks, ornate mats for sleeping or processing sago, and the most fascinating of the rattan products—simple bracelets, given as gifts or merely exchanged between friends. A *selungan* is fashioned from twisted rattan fiber,

blackened with the sap of a plant, and buried overnight in the mud of the watering hole of a wild boar. The *jong* is a more elaborate bracelet, a band of rattan with a golden hue, etched with designs that ensure that the dreams of the carver fuse with those of the recipient. ❧

 This monkey— when I was walking, I heard the noise of many monkeys, krraa, krraa, and I looked up—an eagle—I saw this monkey, and I caught him, and that's how I came to raise him. At first he would say *unyah, unyah, hoh, hoh;* he was still wild and afraid. Now he is tame, and they can bring him along when they go to make sago.

RÉMEN PAREN
Ubong River
May 1993

Paren Jemerai, Rémen's father, resting at the trailside.

Lejeng with her macaques.

One day when Rémen (my son) was out hunting, he saw an eagle that had caught a baby monkey. And this baby monkey escaped from the bird, and then Rémen caught it. And Rémen returned, and I heard the sound of this monkey, and I was happy, and I took it and I fed it. And I was so happy.

Even though I already have three monkeys, I'm still trying to get more because I really love animals. I still want to get more. And even though I am not strong, when I am on the trail and I look at my animals, they make me strong again, they give me the strength to walk on again. There were some people before who had a really huge monkey, as big as a human, really excellent. I'd love to have a monkey as big as that. And it was fat, and its teeth were long. It was a really fine monkey.

Even if our domestic animals are fat and healthy, we still never kill them and eat them. If we happen to kill a mother animal in the forest, we will eat it; but

once we have made her baby into a pet, we will never eat it, no matter how fat and healthy it may become. We never eat animals that we have raised because we think of them as our own children. And our pet animals that die, even if they are fat, we will not eat them; we make them a grave in the forest. And sometimes when they die, we weep for them, just as we would weep for a human being; that is why we don't want to eat them. And from our origins, we have never eaten our domestic animals. Our parents and our grandparents never ate their pets, and so we won't eat ours. And when they are alive, they live with us, and sometimes they even eat with us, so that's why we can't eat them when they are dead.

With all these animals of ours, when we go out for food, we bring them food, like sago and fruits. And when some fruits are ripe, they are very happy, and they climb up to them, and they drop them down to us, and we eat them down here

on the ground, and we're very content because it is they who climb up for them. And also, when we go out walking with our animals, like the long-tailed macaques and the pig-tailed macaques, it's really good, and we're very glad to have them along because they are like people, and they climb up and get fruits for us to eat down here on the ground. When we are walking, if we should come across a snake, or something else that is dangerous, they will discover it before we do, and so we're lucky because in this way they protect us from harm. And if we should encounter evil people, either in front of us or behind us, they notice them first because their eyes are very sharp, and their hearing is good, too, so they notice right away. These are some of the benefits we get from our animals.

LEJENG KUSIN
Ubong River
May 1993

 We are happy when we see them eating, we are happy when we see them follow us when we are out walking. No matter where we go—even if we cross a river, they will cross the river after us. They are good at following us. They are just like dogs, all these animals that we keep. This is not just in recent times that we raise these animals; long-tailed macaques, pig-tailed macaques, deer, pig, even birds, we raise them from when they are small to when they are old, like birds—we raise them, and when they are big, they will take wing, they will fly far away, yet they will return by themselves. They will fly

away, yet they will return by themselves. Until they die, or until they run away, we will not eat them.

As far as wild animals in the forest go, we hunt them with blowpipes, we shoot them with shotguns, this we can do. If they are still alive, and we carry them back to the house, we will not eat them. The ones that die right away back there in the forest, those are the only ones that we will eat. If an animal is alive and is brought back to the house, we immediately treat it as if we had raised it ourselves.

RÉMEN PAREN
Ubong River
May 1993

IAN MACKENZIE

*With no tradition of writing,
the Penan use sign sticks to
communicate in the forest.*

As the Penan move across their forested landscape, often spending long periods alone or in small family groups, a most extraordinary dialogue is maintained between disparate parties by means of sign sticks, branches or saplings strategically placed and decorated with symbols that convey specific messages. The symbols are not universal, but are understood by members of the wide-ranging nomadic community. These sign sticks, known to the Penan as *oroo*, can indicate where and when a party has split up, the direction each group has traveled, the anticipated length of the journey, the difficulty of the terrain, and whether or not food is available. On the sign stick shown on this and the facing page, a stitched leaf pierced by a dart indicates that a wild boar has been killed. The folded leaf is the sign for "hunger." The dart in the unfolded leaves reveals that birds have been shot. The two twigs of equal length affirm that the forest is free of intruders and that all Penan are of one heart. The seedlings represent "house" or "shelter." The twig, carved in the form of a screw and planted obliquely in the ground, points in the direction that the sign maker is traveling. Interpreting these symbols requires both a knowledge of their individual meanings and an understanding of the context in which the message was left. This particular sign stick encourages a slower party of Penan to catch up with a group of hunters, stay in their shelter, and share in a meal of birds and wild boar. ❧

DAVID HISER • PHOTOGRAPHERS / ASPEN

IAN MACKENZIE

Paren Jemerai with a
seperut, *a talisman used to*
repel malevolent spirits.

The Penan, like many indigenous peoples, believe that spirits are ultimately responsible for sickness and misfortune. Simple ceremonies led by spirit mediums known as *dayong* are held to appease the forces of darkness and exorcise the body of the afflicted. The sources of malevolence and disease are several. *Penakoh* is a malicious and vengeful spirit that may seek refuge in the trunk of the strangling fig. A master of deceit and disguise, *Penakoh* lurks in the form of animals or demons, ready to betray the living. The wrath of other spirits is felt by those who ignore the omen birds or violate taboo by killing trees.

Penan must be particularly careful in all matters related to the dead. Never will they remain in a camp where death has stalked, nor will they mention the name of a dead person. To do so would be to incur certain misfortune. Hence the Penan use a complex system of death names not only to refer to those who have died but also to align the living with the deceased. Some groups of Penan, for example, refer to the dead by adding the prefix *dulit* to the name of the place where the person died. Other Penan refer to the dead as *mukun*, a word that normally means aged and implies weakness and decrepitude. Among the Western Penan, the naming prohibition extends to animals as well. A live wild boar is called *babui*, but once killed it is referred to as *kan*, which simply means meat.

opposite:
The nocturnal tarsier. Its
haunting appearance has
made it an object of dread.

For the Penan, death is the first teacher, the first pain, the edge beyond which life as they know it ends and wonder begins. Possessing no digging tools, the nomadic Penan do not bury their dead. Instead, the bodies are wrapped in mats and laid with a few personal effects in the forest, perhaps beside a tree, by a waterfall, between two boulders, or alongside a stream or some other landmark with which the deceased was familiar in life. Occasionally the dead are placed on platforms to protect them from animals, or left in the abandoned *lamin* where they died, to await dissolution amid the decaying ruins of their former shelter. In the aftermath of a death, the survivors move on, threading their way through the forest to another site long visited by their kin group, and ready once again to be occupied. For several weeks it is considered taboo to return to the place of death. Through time, each of these points of tragedy drifts from memory into the realm of myth, and gradually becomes part of a landscape upon which the entire genealogy of the people is written. ❦

The demon Penakoh *dwells within the strangler fig. Dispersed by birds, the fig seeds germinate high in the crown of a forest tree. As the plant grows, it sends down roots which gradually envelop and ultimately kill the host. In time the original tree decays, leaving a cavernous space among the many trunks of the free-standing fig.*

SPIDERHUNTER BIRD, SEND OUT WILD BOAR

Come spirit of speed,
Come Spiderhunter bird,
Send out wild boar easily seen,
Give them to me on the mountain,
Fulfill my wish, O Kingfisher bird,
Give me boar when I go hunting.

Hunting prayer of the Western Penan
Collected by Carol Rubenstein

Completely dependent on the forest for food, the Penan are widely acknowledged by other Dayak peoples as being the best trackers and hunters. In seeking large game such as deer or wild boar, the Western Penan use dogs, and they slay their prey with spears. The Eastern Penan also keep dogs, but only as pets. Both groups now have primitive shotguns, often homemade, but for birds and smaller animals such as monkeys, the blowpipe remains the weapon of choice. A marvel of indigenous technology, the blowpipe, or *keleput,* is lighter than a shotgun. Manufactured from forest materials, it uses ammunition that is readily replaced. The darts kill silently, allowing a hunter in certain instances to drop several animals or, alternatively, to take a second shot should the first miss. Though less effective than a shotgun in the dense undergrowth of a secondary forest, the *keleput* is unsurpassed in efficiency in the open primary forest.

On sighting prey, the Penan hunter becomes still, and then begins a series of slow, cautious movements. A poisoned dart, taken from the bamboo quiver lashed to his waistband, is inserted into the mouthpiece. Holding the weapon steady, with both hands cradling one end, the hunter takes a shallow breath and then pauses to take final aim. The accuracy of these weapons is such that targets the size of a small leaf may be struck from seventy-five feet; small birds are readily taken from the canopy of the forest. Superb hunters, the Penan sometimes load two darts into the blowpipe, firing them in rapid succession with two blasts of the same breath. Once an animal has been struck, the poison takes effect quickly. How long the prey survives depends both on its size and on the potency of the particular batch of poison. Birds may die within minutes. Larger animals are stalked cautiously until they succumb. ❦

IAN MACKENZIE

 I was just starting to learn to hunt from my father when he died. So my father had no opportunity to teach me. So I learned from my uncle, using a blowpipe made of bamboo. I started with bats. But I used darts without poison. The reason they don't give you many poisoned darts is safety. Even if one just pricks your skin, you will die. Even if it does not break off, you'll still die.

In the beginning they did not give me many poisoned darts, but as I took more and more *pu'an*, *mega*, *teléé* [three distinct squirrels], they gave me more darts, and they were more potent. So then I worked up to *koyat* and *nyakit* [monkeys] and hunted them successfully. And all the animals that are higher in the trees. Then I went hunting and saw this barking deer. Of course, when you are young, you are not strong enough to blow the darts hard, so after my first shot, the deer ran away, and then it stopped, and so I went in closer, and I blew again. And then it moved just a short distance, and it died. I wasn't big at all. I couldn't even carry the deer. After that, they gave me larger darts. I still did not know how to make the poison.

Only later did I encounter a wild boar. The first *babui* was a really big one. The tusks were big like this. The dart entered the boar, and the boar ran only as far as a place nearby where it had been sleeping, and then it died. I only carried back the internal organs, because it was not possible for me to carry the whole animal. So the adults felt really happy that I was able to kill the boar because they had just thought of me as a young inexperienced child. And so they gave me a quiver, and *keleput mu'un, keleput kebit*, a real blowpipe, a long blowpipe. The blowpipe that I had used to kill the *babui* was just this long.

ASIK NYELIT
Tutoh River
February 1993

A living nyagang *tree that has been harvested for blow-pipe wood.*

Spiderhunter Bird, Send Out Wild Boar

IAN MACKENZIE

Blowpipe making.

Though several plant species may be used to make blowpipes, the preferred material is a hard, dense, straight-grained wood known as *nyagang*. The Penan cut from a living tree a thin length of wood, roughly three inches in diameter and six to eight feet long. A high platform is then constructed for the painstaking process of boring the shaft. Standing on the platform, the carver uses a long, narrow iron rod to drill through the length of the weapon, occasionally pausing to pour water into the hole to float up the sawdust and cool the bore. Once the task is complete, the outside of the weapon is shaped and then given a fine finish with the *bekela* leaf, a botanical substitute for sandpaper. In the final step, the Penan lash a sharp iron blade to the tip so that the weapon may double as a spear.

The blowpipe technology utilizes half a dozen forest plants. The dart quiver is made of bamboo, the darts are fashioned from the stems of various palms, and the cone-shaped plug at the base of the dart, carved to precisely fit the bore of the weapon, is made from the pith of a sago palm. Two types of dart are used. A *tahat* is a straight wooden projectile used primarily to kill small prey—birds, squirrels, lizards, snakes, and frogs and other amphibians. A metal-tipped dart, known as *belat*, is employed for larger game such as monkeys. The poison is applied to the tip of the dart; for reasons of safety, it is not applied to the cutting edge of the *belat*. ❧

Spiderhunter Bird, Send Out Wild Boar

 There are two stories about the origins of *tajem* [the dart poison]. One says that long ago, before the great flood and the great earthquake, the people saw a cobra biting the bark of a tree. They knew that the cobra was poisonous, and they wondered if there was some connection. So they cut into the bark of that tree, and took some of the latex, and found that it could kill. That is how they learned about *tajem*.

The other story is about a woman who had two suitors. She loved them both, but knew she could not marry them both. So instead she turned herself into a *tajem* tree so that they could both share her.

ASIK NYELIT
Ubong River
May 1993

IAN MACKENZIE

The Penan begin the process of making *tajem* by cutting a v-shaped incision into the bark of a tall forest tree scientifically known as *Antiaris toxicaria*. The latex, which collects in a length of bamboo, is later placed in a container made of leaves and slowly heated to evaporate the excess fluid. Once the poison achieves a thick, viscous consistency, it may be applied to the darts, which are then carefully dried. Alternatively, the poison may be poured into leaf molds to harden for later use. Stored in bamboo containers and kept cool, the preparation retains its potency for a year or more.

The active ingredient is an extremely toxic cardiac glycoside called *antiarin*. Unlike *curare*, a muscle relaxant from the Amazon that kills by causing suffocation, cardiac glycosides interfere with the normal functioning of the heart, precipitating lethal arrhythmia. Both *curare* and *tajem* are nontoxic if swallowed. For the poisons to work, they must enter the bloodstream. The technique the Penan use to make the poison is relatively straightforward. Their discovery, however, that this orally inactive substance, derived from a single tree in a vast forest of thousands of species, can kill when administered intramuscularly is profound.

The Penan maintain that the strength of the poison varies, both from tree to tree and within a single individual, depending

Extracting latex from a tajem, or dart poison, tree.

WADE DAVIS

on the time of day and the season in which the latex is gathered. The strength of a given preparation must be empirically tested by hunting. Should the poison prove insufficiently toxic, the Penan will augment the preparation with various admixtures—roots and stems, leaves, rhizomes, and bark of plants belonging to unrelated families, only some of which are known to contain pharmacologically active constituents. The admixtures are generally employed in very small quantities, burned to ash or merely ground from fresh material. Their exact chemical role is uncertain; some, no doubt, are added for their magical properties. The rhizome of *long*, for example, a terrestrial member of the philodendron family, is said to ensure that the prey will not feel the impact of the dart. *Laka* is a parasitic plant. *Binah*, *sekaliu*, and *telikut* are trees. *Tajem moséng* is a very rare liana, and *basong* is a ginger. A small piece of the root of the climbing liana *tuak*, burned to ash and added to *tajem*, is considered to be particularly toxic. If improperly prepared, however, *tuak* is said to weaken the poison.

Scientific understanding of the Penan dart poison is limited due to a lack of ethnobotanical data and the Penan's close guarding of information about it. The toxic effects of the principal poison may indeed be enhanced by the addition of subsidiary ingredients; this is an important feature of many folk preparations around the world. Different chemical compounds in relatively small concentrations may effectively potentiate each other. The result is a powerful synergistic effect, a biochemical illustration of the whole being greater than the sum of the parts. ❧

The Penan recognize and eat more than thirty species of fish. These they gather in small streams, in pools cut off by the falling water level of the dry season, or in slow-moving river backwaters. To fish, they often employ biodegradable toxins that they derive by crushing the leaves, stems, roots, and fruits of as many as a dozen forest plants. Placed in water, these plant materials release chemicals that interact with the gills, inhibiting respiration and ultimately causing death by suffocation. The stunned fish float to the surface and are easily gathered. The environmental impact of these plant toxins is slight and localized, and their use, if done in moderation, does not cause permanent harm to the aquatic ecosystem.

In many instances, particularly when fishing along the banks of rivers or in broad stretches of water, the Penan use throw nets acquired by trading. Many of the fish they go after are fruit eaters, dependent on the trees that overhang the streams. To catch these fish, the Penan toss small pebbles to mimic the falling fruit, and then cast their nets as the fish rush to the decoy. The timber industry in Sarawak typically logs to the edges of streams, eliminating the fruit-bearing trees. Though it has not been confirmed scientifically, the Penan maintain that the crushed remains of the forest plants, deposited on a massive scale, cause further harm, choking the rivers with poisons. 🌿

Spiderhunter Bird, Send Out Wild Boar

When I first started hunting wild boar, I went out into the forest. I kept going farther into the forest, looking for their tracks. When I went farther into the forest, and saw many fresh footprints, I knew there were fruits nearby, and that the *babui* were going to visit the fruit trees.

The only thing I had brought with me was a small basket. That was the only thing I was carrying, because I was just a little boy. I kept my *tahat* darts inside the basket; I did not have a quiver. I was only planning to hunt for birds. My father had given me a *belat* dart in case I should meet with a dangerous boar or bear. That's why our parents gave them to us. They don't give those out for just any old reason; a kid might prick himself and die.

I came across a *babui*. The boar was so close. Because I was so small, just the size of a monkey, the *babui* did not notice that I was there. I shot the *belat*, but it did not enter the animal very far. But the *tajem* was good, and the *babui* only ran for a short distance, as far as that campfire there, and then it died. So it was lucky that I had brought the *belat* dart that had been prepared by my father.

The *babui* was too big for me to carry, so I went home to get someone to fetch it. At first the adults said, *"Kenyo!* You're lying! There are no *babui* near here." But I had brought back the boar's tail. Only when I showed it to them did they believe me.

TU'O PEJUMAN
Tutoh River
February, 1993

DAVID HISER • PHOTOGRAPHERS / ASPEN

Although the Penan hunt hornbill and monkeys, sambar deer, gibbons, mouse deer, civets, squirrels, and a host of other creatures, their principal source of meat is *babui*, a variety of bearded boar endemic to Borneo. Usually active by night, the omnivorous bearded boar lives on a diet of fallen fruits and seeds, roots, leaves, insects, worms, and other small animals. Variable in color and characterized by a long muzzle with many bristles, the bearded boar is a formidable adversary, weighing as much as 250 pounds.

Penan hunters, traveling alone or with a single companion, pursue *babui* by day or night. Once the animal is killed, shoulder straps made from rattan are passed through its hide. The carcass is then hoisted onto the hunter's back and carried to camp. The animal is butchered, with equal portions being allotted to each family. The perishable internal organs are roasted and consumed immediately. Whatever meat cannot be eaten fresh is cubed and dried over a fire. The fat, a valuable trade item, is rendered by the women and stored in sealed three-foot lengths of bamboo.

The significance of *babui* and other wild game in the diet of the Penan and other Dayak peoples of Sarawak is considerable. The International Union for the Conservation of Nature and Natural Resources (IUCN) has estimated that indigenous peoples annually harvest over a million wild boar, 23,000 sambar deer, and 31,000 barking deer, a total of approximately 18,000 tons of wild meat, valued conservatively at U.S. $80 million. Replacing this protein source with domestic boar or beef would cost the Malaysian society more than U.S. $123 million each year. For the Penan, who have no tradition of animal husbandry, healthy populations of wild prey are critical to the survival of their culture. The loss of the wild boar would reduce them to a shadow of what they now are.

In recent years the dramatic increase in logging activity has coincided with a serious reduction in the availability of wild game. A study conducted by the World Wildlife Fund suggests that among indigenous peoples annual per capita protein consumption has dropped from 120 to 26 pounds. A Sarawak government study acknowledges that in recently logged areas there has been among Dayak peoples a threefold increase in malnutrition.

The causes of the decline in boar populations are several. *Babui* normally travel alone or in small groups, moving seasonally from one area to another in response to the fruiting cycle of the forest trees. In regions of pri-

mary forest, and in years of unusually heavy crops of wild seeds and fruit, migratory herds of as many as a million wild boar have roamed the land in search of food, crossing broad rivers and traversing mountain ranges. After an area is logged, their food supply is reduced because many of the commercially extracted species—*meranti, kapur,* and others—produce copious amounts of fruit. Smaller boar populations do

adapt to secondary growth and survive in fragmented patches of forest. Hunting pressure, however, is severe, uncontrolled, and exasperated by the extensive network of logging roads that dissects the forest. For recreation and to augment their wages by selling meat, employees of the logging companies, traveling by open truck and armed with high-powered rifles, shotguns, and searchlights, hunt by day and night, often driving local populations of *babui* to extinction. ❧

If we go hunting, we go on foot. But the people from the camps, the loggers, they have trucks. At night they can go out in their trucks, and use torches. They shoot anything they see. This scares all the animals and drives them all away. It's really hard for us to hunt them then.

MUTANG TU'O
Ubong River
May 1993

On the logging roads, it's really hard for us to hunt. It's really hard to hunt up there because there's so much thick undergrowth and there are landslides, and there are a lot of felled trees. It's really hard for us to hunt, it's really hard for us to see anything because of the thick new growth and the fallen branches. If you go to hunt there, it's easy to make a noise, and the animals run away. And if there's a bear, if there's a snake, it's really hard for us to penetrate that thick growth and pursue them. As for me, even if I apply all my skill, in a place like that it's really very difficult. It's very difficult for me to get big animals, or even small animals.

My father used to tell me of the old days, about our life when we used to hunt in the old days. In one minute, even in one second, we would find animals when we went hunting, wherever we went. Whenever we were hungry, whenever we wanted to eat, we would find animals right away. In just a minute we would find animals. And this is what my father said. When we went looking for barking deer, or wild boar, or sago, or anything that we wanted in the forest, it was so easy to get.

ASIK NYELIT
Ubong River
May 1993

KINGFISHER, GIVE ME MUCH SAGO

O Kingfisher,
give me much sago,
give me enough to eat my fill.
Kingfisher, bless us with sago abundant,
bless us with taro, cassava, banana
O Kingfisher, now I go forth to chop sago,
Let my basket be filled,
filled to bursting,
O Kingfisher.

> Song of the Western Penan
> Collected by Carol Rubenstein

Though hunting and fishing are prevalent in many indigenous societies, it is almost always agriculture, the source of basic carbohydrates, that anchors a people to a particular place in a landscape. What has allowed the Penan to remain nomadic is the existence of a remarkable group of wild palms known collectively as sago.

The principal source of sago is *uvud, Eugeissona utilis,* a species commonly found in dense groves on hillsides and ridges throughout the Penan territory. Each tree consists of multiple shoots; normally only one of these is harvested at a time. To ensure that the plant will continue to thrive, great care is taken to avoid damaging the roots. Once the trunk has been felled, it is cut into manageable sections and carried to an appropriate place for processing, generally a stream or a nearby body of water. The sections of trunk are split longitudinally and the soft pith is pounded and frayed with a wooden mallet. The fibrous pulp is placed on a finely woven rattan mat that rests on a raised frame. It is then kneaded with the feet. Water, poured over the frame, mixes with the starch, which then filters through the rattan and settles as a thick white paste on the surface of a lower mat. The starch is later dried over a fire to produce the actual sago flour. The process can be completed in a single day. Depending on the species used and the means of preparation, sago has a taste and texture ranging from bland and glutinous to rich and meaty.

Gathering sago is the purest expression of Penan life. It is the practice that keeps them in motion, and the means by which they mark points of memory in a densely forested land. It is the adaptation that frees them from the constraints of the planted seed. Rice cultivation, by contrast, requires exhaustive work, months of waiting, and permanent settlements with adequate granaries for storage. Gathering sago is one of the world's most efficient ways of securing food: in a single day, a Penan family can produce enough sago starch to feed itself for a week. If leisure time is a measure of affluence, the nomadic Penan are among the richest people on earth.

IAN MACKENZIE

Extracting starch from the wild sago palm.

One of the remarkable aspects of the use of sago among the nomadic Penan is the fact that the starch produced by an individual is invariably shared among all families in the encampment. The division of game is hardly surprising. Meat readily spoils and inevitably certain hunters are more accomplished than others. But anyone can make sago, and the dry flour can be stored almost indefinitely. There is no compelling material imperative to share. In the case of sago, it is the gesture itself that matters, an act of grace that binds the people into a single community. ❧

A pet macaque eating sago.

DAVID HISER • PHOTOGRAPHERS / ASPEN

Ukun Kusin prepares sago.

Kingfisher, Give Me Much Sago

Such a shame, your flesh is not accustomed to being split by us,
Such a shame, you're not accustomed to being eaten by us,
You're not accustomed to being cooked by us.
Such a shame, you'll never see your shoot grow,
You're not accustomed to being taken away.
Such a shame, you never had to deal with us before,
Such a shame, you weren't accustomed to people in the old days.
Oh Sago, you were not accustomed to such things.
Such a shame, you were never accustomed to people,
you were never accustomed to the grownups of the past.
Oh Sago, you were not accustomed to such things.
Such a shame, you are not accustomed to being cooked,
to your flesh being eaten.
Such a shame, you were never accustomed to people being
    angry with you.
You are not accustomed to going rotten now,
It's not like life in the old times.
You are not accustomed to being treated like this.
Such a shame, you weren't accustomed to being sliced up like
    this in the old days.

A song by **IBAU JIKI**, a boy of eight, sung while
cutting *sin uvud*, the fresh heart of the sago palm.
Ubong River
April 1993

*Ibau Jiki, grandson of Wéé
Salau.*

opposite:

*Ukun Kusin and her
husband, Wéé Salau.*

Here, even if a
little child goes
hunting, he'll
come back with meat; even
if a little child goes to find
sago, he'll come back with
sago. This makes us feel
happy. We have never had
a bad life here, we have
never wanted for food here,
there has always been food
in abundance. The forest is
like a shop because there's
always food for us in the
forest. At the longhouse
they have to plant food
before they can eat; here,
we don't have to plant, it's
much easier, there's always
food for us in abundance.
The food that they plant at
the longhouses often runs
out; but here, our food can
never run out. And we are
always happy, for there is
clear water, and the forest
is always a delight to us.
And here, even when it
rains and it is cold, we are
still happy. And thus our
life has been since our
origins.

LEJENG KUSIN
Ubong River
May 1993

The forests of the Penan produce a veritable cornucopia of wild fruits, some of which may be new to science. Although a complete study of Penan ethnobotany has yet to be undertaken, it is known that the Penan harvest and consume more than a hundred wild fruits, numerous species of fungi, and many types of wild greens and edible palms.

Though all food in a Penan encampment is distributed equally among the different families, it is nevertheless the custom to invite anyone lingering in the vicinity of a shelter to join in any meal. Failure to accept the invitation is not only considered impolite, it is a gesture that actively invokes the wrath of a dark spirit known as *Ungap*. Curiously, it is the host, not the offending guest, who is endangered by this violation of etiquette. The result will be an accident, a laceration with a bush knife, or possibly a frightening encounter with a cobra. Perhaps more than any other example, this social obligation underscores the degree to which reciprocity is valued as a fundamental ethic in Penan society. ❧

But as for us, the Penan people, we don't want to eat pet animals like that. And at Easter, if we go to a longhouse, we don't want to eat. Sometimes we close our mouths, we close our noses. We don't want to smell the stink of the pet pigs, or buffalo, or chickens that they murder. We just go to the service, but don't stay and eat the pet animals they serve at the meal. And when we see a dish that has been prepared from a cow, or from a chicken, we feel the same as if it were a dish prepared from human flesh. We don't think of it as animal flesh, but as human flesh, because it has been kept and raised by humans. When we look at it we feel like we want to vomit, we just don't want to eat it.

LEJENG KUSIN
Ubong River
May 1993

I would rather see them eating McDonald's hamburgers than the unmentionables they eat in the jungle.

ABDUL RAHAM YAKUB
Former Chief Minister of Sarawak

The Penan pursue wild game but never eat domesticated animals.

NOMADS OF THE DAWN

We'd like to take them out of the jungle. Give them a decent modern living. . . . Now at this point there are about three hundred odd of these Penan still resisting to come out of the jungle. . . . I mean we're talking about 1992! We're talking about the twenty-first century! We can't afford to have some of our population still hunting monkeys.

RAFIDAH AZIZ
Malaysian Minister of International Trade and Industry
May 1992

We don't want them running around like animals. Shouldn't they be taught to be hygienic like us and eat clean food?

JAMES WONG
Sarawak State Minister of the Environment and Tourism

 The government always says that the Penan eat dirty things, that we do not eat well. The government always says this. But now you, yourself, have seen. Each time that we eat, we clean our pans, we clean our cooking pots, we clean our plates that are dirty. We are not like animals, we do not eat any old thing that's lying around. The government says the reason it is trying to give development to the Penan, the reason that it is trying to change the way we live, is to make us clean like other people. But when they speak in this way, they lie! When they speak like this, their words are not true! They speak these words only out of their desire, their eagerness, to destroy our forest, the forest of the Penan. That is the reason that they utter such words. But these words are not true, as you yourself now know.

WÉÉ SALAU
Baa' Bila
April 1993

Lighting the hearth fires.

For the Penan the bounty of the rain forest is by no
means limited to the foods they eat or the plants they
transform into tools and shelter. Perhaps the most remarkable
evidence of their understanding and powers of observation is
found in their extensive use of medicinal plants. In any area of
the forest a Penan elder will readily find a score of healing
agents—herbs and roots, the rhizomes of ferns, crushed
leaves, and the bark of trees and of the lianas that hang from
the heights of the canopy. Plants are administered as antidotes
for food poisoning, contraceptives and abortifacients, clotting
agents, general tonics and stimulants, disinfectants, and medicines to set bones, eliminate parasites, and treat headache,
fever, lacerations, boils, snakebite, toothache, diarrhea, skin
infections, and rashes. There are magical plants employed to
dispel evil spirits, stop babies' crying, and empower hunting
dogs. Many Penan medicinal plants have several uses.
Getimang, for example, is one of the plants employed as an
antidote to the dart poison. The petiole of the same plant is
chewed as a treatment for stomachache and indigestion. The
leaves, heated over a fire, repel mosquitoes and keep bees
away during honey gathering. The peeled inner bark is said to
relieve headache when applied to the forehead. In the absence
of a thorough ethnobotanical study, which has never been permitted by the Sarawak government, it is impossible to know
which of these plants may be pharmacologically active and
which mere supports for sympathetic magic.

According to the World Health Organization, roughly 90

A remedy for headache.

percent of the people in developing countries rely chiefly on traditional medicine for their primary health care needs. This high degree of dependence, together with many thousands of years of experimentation, have yielded numerous plants of true pharmacological worth.

Plants are useful as medicines because they have evolved complex secondary compounds and alkaloids as chemical defenses against insect predation. These defensive chemicals, which in certain plants may comprise 10 percent of dry weight, can be exploited by science for therapeutic purposes. In seeking new medicines from the forest, ethnobotanists recognize that the difference between a poison, a medicine, and a narcotic is often just a matter of dosage. Thus their primary goal is to identify any plant that is pharmacologically active. The key element in this process of drug discovery is the knowledge of indigenous peoples. Seventy-five percent of the biologically active plant-derived compounds currently in use worldwide were discovered in a folk context, the gifts to the

modern world of the shaman and the witch, the healer and the herbalist, the magician and the priest.

Tragically, the medicinal knowledge of the Penan, a resource potentially of global significance, is being compromised by the day. Logging activities are destroying the source of the medicines even as the forces of acculturation undermine the legitimacy and integrity of the folk tradition. Understaffed government clinics and itinerant physicians who make rare and brief appearances in the Penan settlements are no substitute for an ancient system of medicine inspired by the spirit of plants and imbued by the people themselves with the power to heal. ❧

Self-inflicted contusions, a treatment for influenza.

DAVID HISER • PHOTOGRAPHERS / ASPEN

 When I was young, my mother would find medicines in the forest. My father and mother would get plants to heal me when I was sick. If someone was injured, they would find medicines, and they would always know where to look for them. It is not the same living here on the riverbank, for those who have children nowadays. The house may be good, but when the children get sick, they cannot get medicine from the forest. If they are sick, they do not have the resources to buy medicine. In the old times, when the forest was intact, the mothers and fathers would look for birds and squirrels, and animals that are good for children.

UNYANG WAN
Long Iman
May 1993

 In former days, even though there was no doctor, no one to give us medicine, we still lived. We knew how to live, even though there was no doctor. The forest gave us medicine. Thus we lived from former days up to the present. The forest gave us all we needed for life, to give life to women, to give life to children. But today, if a woman or a child, if a mother or a wife, should die, they say, "Oh, it's because you didn't go to the doctor."

But there is a problem. If we are sick, and go to the hospital, or go to meet the doctor, we have to go way upriver. How can we go to the doctor? We have to pay to get there. We don't have the stamina. We are just human. Sometimes a person who is very ill will die before reaching the hospital. But if we still have the forest, we can help ourselves, there is no need to travel far. We can heal ourselves, we can find the medicines we need in the forest.

ASIK NYELIT
Baa' Bila
April 1993

Ukun Kusin gathering the leaves of nyavung, *which are ground and boiled to produce a remedy for headache and fever.*

Each morning at dawn the gibbons howl and their voices carry for great distances, riding the thermal boundary created by the cool of the forest and the warm air above as the sun strikes the canopy. Penan never eat the eyes of the gibbons. They are afraid of losing themselves in the horizon. They lack an inner horizon. They don't separate dreams from reality. If someone dreams that a tree limb falls on a camp, they will move with the dawn.

BRUNO MANSER
a Swiss national who lived six years with the Penan
Honolulu
June 18, 1990

At twilight the sky over the forest is darkened by columns of bats that emerge from the earth by the millions and stream away into the night.

CHRIS NOBLE

THE RED EARTH

The biodiversity of tropical rain forests is astounding. An acre or two of temperate woodland usually contains no more than a dozen tree species. In the tropics the same area of land may support as many as three hundred. The insect fauna in the tropical rain forests has been estimated to include a staggering thirty million species. One entomologist found more kinds of ants in a single tropical tree stump than had been reported for all of Great Britain. Another found twelve hundred different beetles in the crowns of nineteen individuals of a single species of tree. A single square mile of tropical rain forest may support twenty-three thousand forms of life.

Represented within the traditional Penan homeland are all the major forest types to be found in the interior of Borneo. These forest communities contain a remarkable number of endemic species. In Borneo no fewer than fifty-nine genera and 34 percent of all plant species are found only on the island. The fauna includes thirty unique birds and thirty-nine endemic terrestrial mammals, as well as scattered populations of rare and endangered animals such as the Sumatran rhino and the orangutan. One entomologist working in Borneo identified some six hundred species of butterflies and caterpillars in a single day. Another reported over a thousand species of cicadas. Botanical studies in the heart of Penan territory have identified over two thousand flowering plants including 120 species of palm, many of which are new to science. In a collection of four thousand fungi, a mycologist found that over half were unknown species. Vegetation surveys have yielded similarly impressive results. In the lowland mixed dipterocarp forests, botanists have discovered a floristic diversity surpassing the most prolific areas of the Amazon. In a series of ten sample plots, each covering 2.2 acres, one botanist counted over seven hundred species of trees, as many as have been recorded for all of North America.

This lush ecosystem is maintained by a complex process of nutrient recycling. In the temperate zone, the periodicity of the seasons results in the accumulation of rich organic topsoils, which serve as a reservoir for up to 80 percent of the nutrients of the ecosystem. In the tropical forest, by contrast, the biological wealth is stored in the living canopy. With constant high humidity and annual temperatures hovering around 80 degrees Fahrenheit, bacteria and microorganisms break down plant matter virtually as soon as the leaves hit the forest floor. With the aid of microbial fungi, a complex mat of tiny rootlets absorbs the nutrients, which are immediately recycled into the forest itself, an exceedingly complex mosaic of thousands of interacting and interdependent forms of life.

To understand the implications of this nutrient regime, one need only scratch the surface of the forest floor. Ninety percent of the roots do not penetrate farther than five inches into the ground. In the absence of deep root systems, many of the largest forest trees are supported by immense buttresses that flare out from the base of the trunk. The reason for these adaptations is the virtual absence of organic soil. In any other part of the world, these lands might be deserts. Only rainfall and temperature, and the rapid manner in which nutrients are recycled, insulate the forest from the poor quality of the soil and permit the luxuriant growth. When an emergent tree blows over, it cuts a swath in the forest, leveling dozens of smaller trees and dragging with it many others. The opening created in the canopy is rapidly exploited by myriad sun-tolerant plants. This process, by which old trees die and new saplings emerge, is part of the natural cycle of the forest and cannot be compared to the ravages exacted on the land by the logging activities of humans.

The industrial removal of the forest cover sets in motion a chain reaction of biological destruction with cataclysmic consequences. Temperatures increase dramatically, relative humidity falls, rates of evapotranspiration drop precipitously, and the mycorrhizal mats that interlace the roots of the forest trees facilitating the absorption of nutrients dry up and die. With the cushion of vegetation gone, the torrential rains create erosion, which leads to further loss of nutrients and to chemical changes in the soil itself. In certain deforested parts of the

The protective coloration of a katydid.

FRANS LANTING • MINDEN PICTURES

opposite:
The blossoms of Rafflesia *are the world's largest flowers, reaching up to three feet in diameter and twenty-eight pounds in weight.*

tropics, the precipitation of iron oxides in leached exposed soils has resulted in the deposition of miles upon miles of lateritic clay, a rock-hard pavement of red earth from which not a weed will grow. In Sarawak, opportunistic plants quickly invade the clearings, growing into a wretched entanglement of half-hearted trees. Whereas the floor of the primary forest is relatively open and easy to traverse, the dense underbrush of the secondary forest can be virtually impenetrable.

The most significant and irrevocable consequence of deforestation is the sacrifice of biological diversity. A conservative estimate of the current worldwide rate of extinction is one thousand species a year, mostly from the loss of forest and other key habitats in the tropics. Within this decade the fig-ure is expected to rise to ten thousand species a year, a rate of one species per hour. During the next thirty years, scarcely longer than the time it takes for a single generation of humans to come of age and give birth, fully one million species may disappear. This spasm of destruction, caused by the folly of one species that is itself entirely dependent on the biosphere, has no precedent in history. 🌿

THOM HENLEY

These jungles are so old they make those in Africa and South America seem merely adolescent by comparison. And the wealth of fauna and flora that inhabit this timeless corner of nature are both strange and exciting to behold. . . . Come to Malaysia and you can experience the wonder of the world's oldest rain forest and her inhabitants.

From an advertisement published by the Malaysian Ministry of Culture, Arts, and Tourism

 In truth, there is no untouched forest. All of the forest, except that part that bears the name "national park," has been finished off by the companies. Here a little remains, only because it has the name "national park." Not because it is an area of the forest that happens to be still untouched.

. . . They have entered our area, they have invaded our rivers, they have made them dirty and muddy, they have trespassed on our forest paths. And up until this very moment we remain weighed down with hardship and poverty. And as I am speaking these words, our life is not good. Surely we live here peacefully, and they have no cause for destroying our forest, they have no cause for destroying our land. They have no cause for making our rivers muddy. They never told us, "Now we are going to demolish your sago, now we are going to destroy your rivers, your hills, your land, your home. Now we are going to obliterate your rattan, and all the other things you get from the forest. All the fruit trees. The place where you Penan live." They never spoke to us thus. Instead, they acted without warning, straightway they destroyed everything.

WÉÉ SALAU
Baa' Bila
April 1993

 They want us to die so that they can take the wood all for themselves. They want the good things for themselves, they don't want to help other people. Improvement and development are just for them, not for anyone else. The only "good thing" that they give us is muddy water and red earth, and the destruction of the forest. That is the only "good thing" they give. Think if we went into the town, and just took things from the shops. If they got angry because we did such a thing, then we, too, should be angry because they are destroying our forests.

ASIK NYELIT
Baa' Bila
April 1993

 If they destroy this place, then they are purposely murdering us, purposely making our life impossible.

LEJENG KUSIN
Ubong River
May 1993

*Niyong La'ing and Ibau Jiki
in the half-light of the forest.*

Today the forests of the Penan are a place of promise and tragedy. As the roads pierce the wild heart of the interior, the Penan find themselves overwhelmed by the frenzy of logging that has gripped Malaysia over the last three decades. The rate of forest destruction is twice that of the Amazon and by far the highest in the world. In 1983 Malaysia accounted for almost 60 percent of the total global export of tropical logs. By 1985, three acres of forest were being cut every minute of every day. With the primary forests of peninsular Malaysia becoming rapidly depleted, the industry turned to Sarawak.

Until 1945 logging in Sarawak was largely restricted to the swamp forests along the coast. After the war, however, the development of portable and efficient chain saws, powerful skidders, bulldozers, and trucks opened up the interior for the first time. By 1971 Sarawak was exporting 4.2 million cubic meters of wood annually, much of it cut from the upland forests of the hinterland. A decade later exports had more than doubled, and by 1985 they had reached 10.6 million cubic meters. In that year over 600,000 acres were logged. An additional 12.7 million acres, representing 60 percent of Sarawak's total forested area, were licensed for future logging. In 1990 the annual cut had escalated to 18.8 million cubic meters. In the Baram River drainage alone, there are today more than thirty logging companies, some equipped with as many as twelve hundred bulldozers, working one million acres of forest on lands traditionally belonging to the Kayan, Kenyah, and

Penan. Within the territory of the Penan alone, 72 percent of the forest is officially designated for commercial exploitation. Most observers consider this figure to be misleading. Evidence on the ground suggests that much of the lowland forest essential to the Penan has already been cut, and what remains is slated to be logged. In 1990 a report published by the International Timber Trade Organization (ITTO), a multinational trade group representing tropical timber producers and consumers in forty-three nations, predicted that by the year 2001, there would be no primary forest remaining in the state.

Logging practices in Borneo in the last decade have plundered an extraordinary natural resource. Waste in the industry has been estimated as high as 50 percent. In December 1983, Tan Sri Ben Stephens, director of the Sabah Foundation, which owns 36 percent of Sabah's remaining unlogged commercial forest, noted that for every cubic meter of wood sold, another cubic meter is cut but discarded. Ninety percent of the wood that is exported leaves Sarawak as unprocessed logs, resulting in a significant loss to the state of revenue and employment. ❧

ANDERSON MUTANG URUD

And if this forest were cut down, if this place were ruined by logging, they wouldn't need to send two or three people here to assault us and kill us. They could send just one person, and he would be strong enough to kill us all for sure. Because we are not used to seeing open spaces, we are not used to seeing trees that have been felled and destroyed. Because there would be nothing left to make us want to live, because the trees we yearn for would have been destroyed. And if they were to say that we were happy, happy in this place after it is logged, it would really mean that they do not want us to live. They do not want us to be happy. They want to assault us and kill us. Surely we do not feel happy or proud about the logging because all these bulldozers, all this logging, is harmful to us. This is our problem, this is our difficulty. We can never be happy living on red ground. And we always feel sad and troubled. When we look at the forest that has been destroyed, we feel the way one feels after not having eaten for a long time.

LEJENG KUSIN
Ubong River
May 1993

The politics of timber in Sarawak begin and end with money. Between 1976 and 1982 the value of timber exported from Sarawak increased from U.S. $138 million to U.S. $525 million. By 1991 the figure was U.S. $1.29 billion. In an economy based almost exclusively on the exploitation of natural resources, and in a region where most of the population remain subsistence farmers, this income represents a staggering concentration of wealth. Far from benefiting the rural poor, however, forest management in Sarawak has been subverted to serve the interests of the ruling elite, who have used their control of the licensing of logging concessions as a political tool, a source of personal wealth, and a means of retaining economic and political power. The authority to grant or deny logging concessions lies strictly with the Minister of Resource Planning. There is no competitive bidding, nor any legal or technical restrictions on who may be awarded a concession. Recipients have included relatives, friends, political associates, and even the Sarawak Football Association.

Between 1970 and 1981, and since 1985, the highly coveted Resource Planning portfolio has been retained in the office of the Chief Minister, the highest authority in the state. Since 1981 the Chief Minister has been Taib Mahmud, a man whose personal fortune, derived from logging, has made him one of the wealthiest men in Malaysia. According to a February 7, 1990, report in the Asian *Wall Street Journal*, "He lives in a well-guarded palatial home in Kuching, and rides in a cream-colored Rolls-Royce. A dapper dresser, he is partial to double-breasted suits and sports a ring with a walnut-sized red gem surrounded by small diamonds."

That his office has been used for personal financial gain became clear during the run up to the state elections in April 1987. At a press conference on April 9, 1987, Taib Mahmud announced the freezing of twenty-five timber concessions totaling 2.75 million acres belonging to relatives and friends of the former Chief Minister, Rahman Yakub. Estimates of the value of these holdings ranged from U.S. $9 billion to U.S. $22 billion. As it turned out, each of Rahman Yakub's eight daughters was the owner of a logging concession. In retaliation for these revelations, Rahman Yakub told the press the names of politicians, friends, relatives, and associates connected with Taib Mahmud who collectively controlled 3.52 million acres of concessions. Ironically, the two antagonists were themselves related: Taib Mahmud was the nephew of Rahman Yakub. Between them, these two quarreling factions of the elite controlled 6.38 million acres, a figure that amounted to over half of all logging concessions and a full third of Sarawak's total forested land. So great is the potential for graft in Sarawak, and so high the financial rewards of securing government office, that politicians have been known to spend as much as U.S. $24 million competing for the support of the 625,000 eligible voters in the state. ❦

 We women feel overwhelmed by a problem that is only getting worse, and when we hear the sound of the bulldozers, all we want to do is cry because the problem we are facing is just too great. And we also cry when we look at the muddy water; how are we going to make our living? The thought of this makes us sorrowful.

LEJENG KUSIN
Ubong River
May 1993

NOMADS OF THE DAWN

Over 98 percent of Sarawak's timber is exported in the form of raw logs, virtually all of it destined for Asian markets. The three largest importers (1989 figures) are Korea (16.4 percent), Taiwan (22 percent), and Japan (46 percent). The role of Japan in the Sarawak timber industry is pivotal. The country depends on Malaysia for more than 85 percent of its tropical wood imports.

Much responsibility for the exploitation of the Borneo rain forests lies far from the shores of Sarawak in the powerful trading houses of Japan. In a 1984 speech on the Sarawak economy, Malaysian Federal Minister Leo Moggie acknowledged that "the marketing of Sarawak timber is still very much controlled by the Japanese trading houses, as Sarawak timber companies are largely dependent on these trading houses for their intricate line of credit." Japanese banks provided the start-up loans for local logging companies. Japanese

companies supply the bulldozers and heavy equipment necessary to extract the logs. Japanese interests provide the insurance and financing for the Japanese ships that carry the raw logs that will be processed in Japanese mills and dispensed as lumber to construction firms often owned by the same concerns that first secured the wood in Sarawak. Once milled in Japan, the wood produced by the oldest and perhaps richest

DAVID HISER • PHOTOGRAPHERS / ASPEN

A Japanese sawmill.

JOSE FUSTE RAGA • ORION

tropical rain forest on earth is employed principally for packaging material, storage crates, and furniture. Roughly half of it is used in construction, mostly as plywood cement forms, which are used once or twice and then discarded.

The Japanese trading companies, or *sogo shosha*, wield considerable political influence and forge close links between industrial investments and foreign aid. In 1987 a scandal surfaced in the Japanese Diet when it was revealed that some $1.5 million of foreign aid funds had been given to Limbang Trading to build logging roads. C. Itoh, one of Japan's nine giant trading companies, owns a major interest in Limbang Trading, the company founded by Sarawak's Minister of the Environment and Tourism, James Wong. The Sarawak government subsequently informed the Japanese that the aid money was needed to construct a school and for roads to service local communities, the very communities whose residents were facing arrest for blockading the logging road expansion. The school in question turned out to have been constructed twenty years before.

Sarawak has consistently maintained that logging operations are both sustainable and intended for the long-term benefit of local communities. The current status of the state forests suggests otherwise. In August 1989, a team from the International Tropical Timber Organization (ITTO) arrived at the invitation of the Sarawak government to investigate logging activities in the state. Their report, expected to vindicate the government's position, instead predicted the exhaustion of the primary forests

TOHAN KOKU SERVICE • ORION

SHIGEO KOGURE • ORION

top:
*Rafts of tropical logs in
Tokyo harbor.*

bottom:
*Tropical hardwood at a
Japanese construction site.*

by the year 2000 and called for an immediate 30 percent reduction in the annual cut. Coming from a conservative organization whose primary concern is maintaining the flow of tropical wood to the international market, this was a stunning condemnation. The Sarawak government responded by increasing the rate of logging 22 percent over the next two years. Finally in December 1991, under increasing pressure from the Malaysian federal government, Sarawak announced that its 1992 production would be 16.2 million cubic meters, an 8.5 percent reduction from the record 1990 harvest of 18.8 million cubic meters. This pledge proved meaningless. By the end of August the entire 1992 quota had already been surpassed.

Aware of diminishing timber supplies, some Malaysian corporations have begun to shift their capital abroad. The giant logging concern Rimbunan Hijau has acquired a dominant place in Papua New Guinea, with 4.94 million acres of concessions in eight provinces. In 1991, the Barama Company secured a deal for a fifty-year license in the South American country of Guyana, where it will exploit some 1.69 million hectares of forests for export. ❦

 There are none of the sounds that we long for, no sound of birds, nor of deer and other animals. The only sound is that of bulldozers, the sound of trucks, and these sounds make us so sorrowful. We certainly do not live happily when we always must listen to the sound of bulldozers and trucks. When we hear the sound of the *merak* bird, the hornbill, the monkeys, the gibbons, and all the other animals in the forest, the ones we eat, when we hear the sounds that they make, then we are happy and satisfied.

These sounds are part of our origins. During the lifetime of our parents we never had to look at red land, we never had to endure the kind of problems we are enduring today. And that is what we always talk about, when we gather together. In the time of our parents we never had these difficulties. That is what we always talk about. When we think of the problems we have today, we feel sad and we cry. If we think of these problems at mealtime, our food loses its taste. And we wonder if there is anyone who can give us comfort, is there anyone who is willing to help us with our problems.

LEJENG KUSIN
Ubong River
May 1993

I will not bow to experts. I am the expert. I was here before the experts were born.

James Wong.

JAMES WONG
Minister of the Environment and Tourism
1988

The environment minister said we don't have to worry about our land being destroyed because whatever we want, even money, will be given to us. I said, "I am not going to take any money from you. Your eyes may fall out of your head to see how much money you have, but I am not going to take any of it."

We are stubborn because we have been living in this area for so long, and our hearts tell us that this is our land. We are not afraid of going to jail because we know that if the logging continues, we are going to die anyway. Tell the timber companies to stop. This is what we want. Only then will we be happy.

Even though we are angry and we say these harsh words, we are like animals that have no teeth. We are like an animal that has no claws. If they continue to extract timber from our forest, our lives will wither like leaves on the trees, like fish without water.

ALONG SEGA
headman,
Long Adang
June 1987

Sarawak has one of the world's most experienced and well-funded forestry departments and, on paper, its forest policy is impressive. Based on the selective logging of carefully managed sites, it strives, at least in principle, to maintain a perpetual supply of wood through the implementation of sustained yield forestry. In practice, however, this policy is exposed as mere rhetoric.

The forests of Sarawak have existed undisturbed for millions of years. They are among the most complex and least understood forests on earth. In the absence of fundamental data on site quality, the growth rates of different tree species, their yields and mortality, their basic biology, and even their taxonomic affiliations, it is difficult to imagine any management strategy being rooted in ecological reality. Sustained yield, an untested hypothesis even in the temperate rain forests, loses all relevance as a scientific concept when applied to an ecological situation the basic parameters of which remain essentially unknown.

In theory, selective logging has far less environmental impact than the clearcut methods employed in temperate rain forests. In contrast to the graphic scenes of desolation that have become such a familiar sight throughout the Pacific Northwest of North America, logged areas of Sarawak remain green and rapidly flush out with secondary vegetation that creates an impression of ecological health. To understand the true impact of selective logging, one must see beyond this illusion, and past the accumulation of well-intended silvicultural theo-

ries that, in effect, mask the difficulty of extracting, in an environmentally sound manner, a few select trees from a given area of tropical rain forest.

On the ground most logging operations in Sarawak occur with little planning and no technical supervision. Decisions on how the trees will be cut and how they reach the specified landing areas lie strictly with the faller and the operator of the bulldozer or skidder. Working on a contract basis, with their wages dependent on production, these men, often poor, uneducated, far from home, and fighting off hunger with a chain saw, place little importance on the environmental implications of their actions. Arriving at a setting, the bulldozer operator establishes a landing and then follows the faller from log to log, skidding them one at a time, expanding his skid trail as the faller works his way deeper into the forest. The faller drops the trees in the direction most convenient to him. To reach them, the bulldozer must work its way throughout the setting, carving long, winding, and even circular tracks into the forest floor. With time at a premium, the bulldozer is constantly in motion, not only hauling logs but moving through the forest locating them. Every activity—turning or lifting the logs to attach the cables, pushing two smaller logs together, maneuvering the bulldozer into place to begin the haul—results in further damage to the forest.

James Wong, former Minister of the Environment and Tourism, and a pioneer in the Sarawak logging industry, does not believe that logging is harmful to the forest. "It has been proven," he has said, "that logged-over areas will return to normal after five years." Most scientific authorities would disagree. Studies published by the UN Food and Agriculture Organization (FAO) and the World Wildlife Fund (WWF) suggest that selective logging as practiced in the hill forests of Sarawak damages 50 percent of the residual stands, removes 46 percent of the natural cover, and seriously damages soils when over 30 percent of the ground surface is exposed. Related studies have concluded that if a mere five trees are fallen per acre, nearly half of the area will be adversely affected. In addition, the construction of roads, landings, and trails permanently alters 12 percent of the total forest area. The estimate for the time necessary for a selectively logged forest to recover is forty years, far less than the twenty-five-year rotation employed in even the most closely managed stands of mixed dipterocarp forest in Sarawak. In many parts of Sarawak, lands that were first logged within the last two decades have, in fact, already been subjected to two and three passes. According to a forestry study published by the World Bank, "There is no documented case of a logged dipterocarp forest actually reverting to its original climax state." ❦

Even though the government is happy destroying the forest, even though the government is happy drinking muddy water, we're not happy drinking muddy water. Although they may be happy, we are not happy.

ASIK NYELIT
Baa' Bila
April 1993

A pristine stream meets a river soiled by logging.

In the old days the water was clean. We just drank straight from the stream. Nobody got sick. Now, if we go to the places the bulldozers have entered, surely we cannot drink the water, because it is muddy. If you drink it, you'll get stomachache, headache. This is the cause of our sickness, all of us, even those of us who live far from the big rivers. . . . In the old days it was so easy to catch fish in this river, in order to feed ourselves. As it is now, we cannot find food.

TU'O PEJUMAN
Tutoh River
February 1993

DAVID HISER • PHOTOGRAPHERS / ASPEN

The cumulative effect of hundreds of bulldozers grinding their way each day through the rain forests of Borneo is one of the most significant environmental problems created by the timber industry. In many logging concessions, skidtrails and landings have laid bare over 40 percent of the forest floor. The extractive process compacts the soil, reducing its capacity to retain water. The removal of vegetation exposes the ground to the direct impact of torrential rains. The result is a dramatically increased rate of erosion, which is further exacerbated by the extent and methods of road construction. With the exception of major haul lines, most logging roads are built with the sole purpose of extracting the timber in the most economical and expedient way. Little attention is paid to drainage or grade. Erosion is chronic.

The most conservative estimates suggest that the removal of the forest canopy results in a thirtyfold increase in soil loss on a given acreage of tropical land. Studies in peninsular Malaysia suggest that soil loss on logged land may be as high as 174 tons per acre per year. Other Malaysian studies indicate that logging operations followed by agricultural exploitation of forest lands may cause a two-hundredfold increase in the sediment load of streams. In the course of just a few years, the indigenous peoples of Sarawak have seen their clear streams choked with sediment. Sixty percent of Sarawak's rivers are now seriously polluted with diesel fuel, sawdust, mud, industrial toxins, and logging debris. The federal government's own five-year plan acknowledges that "soil erosion and siltation have become Sarawak's main water pollution problem." ❧

 We had clearly marked off the grave site of my father on the Keduan River. But the Samling Company did not care—and they simply bulldozed the place. So the company treats us like dogs—as long as you live, they do not care about you, and it is the same when you are dead. It is like our enemy, who wants to kill us, because it destroys all our sago palms and what we need to live, even our grave sites.

SANAM
a nomad of the
Bare River
quoted in *Stimmen aus dem Regenwald*
by Bruno Manser
1992

 This makes our hearts sick. The dead father does not move, and my dead mother cannot cry out.

RAJA JEMALE
Long Palo
quoted in *Stimmen aus dem Regenwald*
by Bruno Manser
1992

In a remarkable inversion of the truth James Wong, himself an owner of a logging concession violating Penan territory, has maintained that "logging is good for the forest." Elsewhere he has identified what he believes is the real cause of Sarawak's ecological difficulties. "It is wrong to say that logging causes serious environmental problems," he has said. "Shifting agriculture causes more destruction than logging."

Swidden, or shifting agriculture, with its cycle of clearing, burning, and planting followed by long periods of regenerative fallow, has long been recognized as one of the most adaptive means of farming in the lowland tropics. Perhaps more than any other agricultural system, shifting cultivation simulates the structure, functional dynamics, and equilibrium of the natural forest. It is the way the settled Dayak peoples have farmed for generations.

Critics of shifting agriculture maintain that the periodic need to cut and burn the forest is inherently wasteful. They measure the life span of a field in terms of the principal crop—usually rice in Sarawak—and suggest that once it can no longer be productively grown, the field must be abandoned. In fact, long after the first two peak years of production, swidden fields continue to yield domestic plant products and a plethora of useful raw materials including medicines, fish poisons, dye plants, insect repellents, body cleansers, firewood, and materials for making thatch, rope, packaging, and crafts.

More importantly, in almost every instance, new swidden fields are cut from secondary growth, not from primary forest.

Evidence from throughout Southeast Asia suggests that in most regions the system of shifting agriculture has remained stable for centuries. In Sarawak, a study conducted by the New York Botanical Garden indicated that the Iban have farmed their areas of settlement for over three hundred years. Contrary to the opinion of James Wong, shifting agriculture is a stable practice dependent less on the destruction of primary forest than on the continual recycling of land occupied for generations. In 1985 in Sarawak shifting agriculture destroyed at most 40,000 acres of primary forest. In the same year industrial logging occurred on 600,000 acres.

That shifting agriculture is the main cause of environmental degradation in Sarawak is a notion maintained and promoted by the highest government authorities. Malaysian Prime Minister Mahathir Mohamad has said, "You are wrong if you think giving the forests to the indigenous peoples will save the trees. The indigenous peoples practice slash-and-burn cultivation, and vast tracts of forest have been completely obliterated by shifting slash-and-burn practice. Logging of selected mature trees allows the forest to regenerate quickly."

In maintaining that swidden agriculture is more destructive than logging, the government shifts responsibility for the current forestry crisis to the indigenous peoples. "Ironically," Evelyne Hong writes in *Natives of Sarawak*, "this attack is led by planners, policy makers, and bureaucrats who are the very people responsible for the wholesale logging of tropical forests." ❧

Before we were happy. Now we have fallen into the hands of the evil Malaysians. They have destroyed the *damar* and the rattan and everything we need in the forest, everything is gone. It doesn't matter where we go. If we go somewhere, the company has already gone there before, and destroyed it. If we go somewhere else, the company has already ruined that area, too. If we went and destroyed their plantations, if we went and destroyed their food, if we went and destroyed their shops, what would they think. Would they be happy if we did that to them?

UKUN KUSIN
Baa' Bila
April 1993

You know from being here. This company is working nearby. Even though we are poor, even though we do not have all the things that we need, I will not allow any of my family members to go and work in the camp. Even if they are thin, even if they are poor. Even if food were scarce, even if our store of food were smaller than a speck of dirt under your fingernail, we would still rely only on our own means to make a living. But as far as the camp is concerned, we will never work there; we will never work there, and in this way we will prove that we do not want these logging companies here.

WÉÉ SALAU
Baa' Bila
April 1993

WADE DAVIS

The Red Earth

PROMISES AND BETRAYAL

 They lie to the white people outside, and they also lie to us. They lie to us here, we who do not know the law. But they also lie to the people outside, who do know the law. And they told us they would hardly take any more wood, they would just take a little bit of wood. But even as we sit here talking, we hear the sound of the bulldozers across the river. They lie, they lie all the time.

ASIK NYELIT
Baa' Bila
April 1993

For thirty years the exploitation of the forests in Sarawak has been justified by a dream of economic development. The timber boom has, in fact, generated massive fortunes and financed a blistering pace of growth. Revenue from the industry accounts for some 50 percent of the state budget. Impressive as this figure may appear, it represents but a token of the total wealth generated by logging. All state revenues are derived from a royalty of only 2 percent of the selling price of the wood. In addition, the timber companies are required to pay federal income tax, but their financial statements often fail to reflect their true earnings. According to the Asian *Wall Street Journal* (February 7, 1990), Rimbunan Hijau, a company operating in Penan territory, generated more than U.S. $750 million between 1976 and 1987 but paid the federal government less than $2 million in taxes. Without doubt, most of the wealth generated by the destruction of the Sarawak forests has been channeled to a small economic and political elite.

There is a hidden cost to the boom that rarely figures in economic forecasts. Though less than 5 percent of the Sarawak work force is employed in logging, the industry in 1983 accounted for 67 percent of all fatal occupational accidents in the state. Three years before that, one worker in five suffered injury and one in four hundred was killed. On the basis of

Promises and Betrayal

injuries reported between 1973 and 1984, it appears that seven lives are lost for every million cubic meters logged in Sarawak. A major injury occurs for every seven thousand cubic meters produced. These figures indicate an accident rate twenty-one times higher than that of the logging industry in Canada. The *New Straits Times* reports that in the last two decades over twenty thousand workers have been killed or seriously injured in the forests of Sarawak.

The forestry sector employs some fifty-five thousand workers and is by far the largest provider of industrial jobs in Sarawak. Given the rate of logging, however, these jobs are destined to disappear along with the trees on which they depend. The liquidation of the forest, and the elimination of the traditional subsistence base, entails the utter and permanent transformation of indigenous cultures. A generation ago virtually all native peoples of Sarawak depended on the forest for their daily needs. Once logging compromised their homelands, the members of many communities became bitterly divided between those who opposed logging and those who felt they had little choice but to join the industrial cash economy. Now, in order to survive, they destroy the land revered by their ancestors. With the imminent demise of the industry, many Dayaks will be forced into a new way of life, the foundations of which have already been laid with the conversion of a number of logged-over areas into oil palm and rubber plantations. The government has already announced ambitious plans for the rapid expansion of this sector of the economy. Thus in many

DAVID HISER • PHOTOGRAPHERS / ASPEN

A Kayan faller in the Penan forest.

parts of Sarawak, the richest and most complex terrestrial ecosystem on earth will be replaced with monoculture. The Dayak peoples, former stewards of the ancient forest and beneficiaries of its bounty, will have no option but to work for outside employers as poorly paid laborers on land that was once their own. ❧

 When we are exposed to the hot sun for even a moment, we are not happy. We are only happy when there is a breeze, when we are under the trees, when we find ourselves in the shade of the forest. And when we must enter the areas that have been logged we are unhappy because it is hot, and it is not suitable for us. We are not happy in a place like that. We are only content when we are in the forest, in a spot like the one we are occupying now. And that is all that we want, to live in a spot like this. If our place here were gone, if our place here were destroyed, it would be the same as if they killed us. If they destroyed this area, it would be the same as cutting our throats, for this is the only place where we can live.

LEJENG KUSIN
Ubong River
May 1993

Describing the donation of used clothing by the Rotary Club of Kuching Central as a positive gesture, Sarawak State Industrial Development Minister Abang Johari Tun Abang Openg said it would go a long way in helping the Penan, who are sensitive to sunlight, when doing their agricultural activities.

The New Straits Times
January 10, 1990

Language is the filter through which the soul of a people reaches into the material world. In Penan the word *tana'* is forest or land, though it also means the world. There are forty words for sago, and no words for good-bye or thank you. In a forest of such abundance, in a culture in which sharing is an involuntary reflex, in a life of endless wandering, certain words have no relevance, certain concepts have no meaning. For the Penan land is a living entity imbued with spiritual meaning and power, and the notion of ownership of land, of fragile documents granting a human the right to violate the earth, is an impossible idea. 🌿

The government says that all the forest land belongs to the government. But Ubong River land belongs to Ubong River Penan. We have everything we need there. Our land guarantees our survival. Why should we go elsewhere? The bodies of our ancestors are buried at Ubong River, so why should we leave them? All we Penan know is that we human beings cannot create land, only God can. If our land at Ubong River belongs to somebody else, we want to ask them, "When did you create the land, or plant the fruit trees, and where are the burial grounds of your ancestors?"

ASIK NYELIT
Marudi
December 1988

Logging camp, Baram River.

WADE DAVIS

For all traditional Dayak peoples, the concept of private ownership of land did not exist. In the agricultural societies customary law dictated that the community as a whole controlled the resource base. Individual proprietary rights were automatically granted to those who worked the land, provided they fulfilled the incumbent ritual and ecological obligations. This principle of land stewardship is enshrined in traditional law or *adat*, a concept that has moral, legal, and religious implications. The subversion of this philosophy, the imposition of a foreign notion of land tenure, and the wresting of control of the land from the indigenous peoples are three dominant themes that have molded Sarawak history since the time of the British.

The benchmark for resource management in Sarawak is the Forests Ordinance of 1953, which divides the land into permanent forests and state land forests. The former were placed under the control and protection of the Forestry Department and expected to satisfy the forestry needs of the state indefinitely. State land forests were to be available for agriculture and other uses. As of 1985, 34 percent, or approximately 12,500 square miles, of Sarawak's 37,000 square miles of forested land had been designated permanent forest. The remainder, some 24,000 square miles, constituted state land forest. In state land forests logging is allowed by permit and there are no restrictions on permissible yields and no management activity by the Forestry Department.

Permanent forests are of three types: forest reserves, protected forests, and communal forests. Forest reserves are set aside as permanent sources of timber. Entry is limited to those licensed for a specific extractive task. Indigenous people are not allowed to harvest or gather any resource of any kind in the forest reserves. In protected forests indigenous customary tenure is similarly forbidden, although indigenous peoples may hunt, fish, and forage, provided they obtain a permit from the Forestry Department. Communal forests are intended to supply the domestic needs of the traditional communities and acknowledge the customary system of land tenure specifically recognized by Sarawak law. Communal forests exist at the discretion of the Minister of Forests, and their designation may be revoked at any time. As of December 31, 1984, communal forests made up only 22 square miles, or 0.17 percent, of Sarawak's permanent forests. As Evelyne Hong writes in *Natives of Sarawak*, "The creation of permanent forests is really to 'protect' large areas of the forests from being claimed by the natives, so that the areas can be made available to logging companies to exploit timber, although in a manner more controlled and regulated than in the free-for-all situation prevailing on the state land forests."

Because Sarawak law technically provides only for the rights of those Dayaks who work the land, the government has consistently maintained that the nonagricultural Penan have no legitimate claim to customary lands and cannot exercise any traditional rights unless they settle down and become farmers. Hence the Penan are placed in the ironic position of having to abandon completely their traditional way of life in order to obtain recognition of their customary rights. ❧

Sago is our food and there is plenty to be found on our land. We Penan of the Ubong River do not eat rice, so why do we need to farm? People in town eat *roti* like their ancestors, so they must farm. They have to rear pigs, chickens, or else buy them, because there are no more animals to hunt in their land, or fish to catch in their rivers, as all of these have died or run away due to the destruction. This is why we Penan do not want our land and forest destroyed.

ASIK NYELIT
Marudi
December 1988

We ask for schools. The government brings tractors. We ask for clinics, they give trucks to bring more logs from the area.

AJANG KIEW
Long Beluk
January 20, 1990

We are asking them to give up their unhealthy living conditions and backwardness for better amenities and a longer and healthier life-style.

MAHATHIR MOHAMAD
Prime Minister of Malaysia
Sarawak Tribune
July 7, 1989

We are not opposed to all change. But we want to choose development based on our needs. A new longhouse like that of the Kayan is fine. But it is not the house of my father, and if it is meant to replace our forest, it means nothing.

DAWAT LUPUNG
Batu Bungan
December 1989

IAN MACKENZIE

Christianity, supported by the political, military, and economic power of the British, began to enter the lives of the Penan some forty years ago. The first missionaries were converted Kenyah from the Upper Baram who contacted the Penan in the Silat River drainage. By 1955 the first Penan had enrolled in Bible school. By 1958 a school had been established. Its first report noted that a group of forty Penan were learning to sing, but regretted that they persisted in singing the same hymn in forty different tunes. By 1985, thirty years after the first missionary efforts, virtually all Eastern Penan had adopted Christianity. Many Western Penan, however, became converts to the Bungan faith, a new religion influenced in part by Christianity and unique to Borneo, which spread into their area in the early 1950s.

The adoption of a new religion seldom results in the complete abandonment of the former belief system. Rather, elements of the old faith are preserved and incorporated into the new. Though many Penan retain their animistic beliefs, Christianity has made them less fearful of malevolent spirits, and many old taboos have fallen away. At one time, for example, hunting expeditions were canceled because of unfavorable bird omens. Now such supernatural warnings are often ignored.

The new faith, though embraced openly by the Penan, has nevertheless corroded important elements of the traditional adaptation. Many omens and taboos, in fact, were vital signs, symbols that taught one how to live in the forest. For all of Penan history, for example, spirits forbade the killing of certain kinds of trees. Under the new order, this taboo has been lifted. The Penan in the settlements find themselves living in houses and sitting in churches constructed of boards sawn from the bodies of their spirits. Christianity has inspired new ways of dealing with the dead, by burial in plots of land adjacent to the *lamin* of the living. Thus one of the motives that for a thousand generations stimulated the Penan to move has been extinguished by a single idea. ❦

Is it right to deny them the advancement of the modern world? Let them choose to live the way they want to live. Let them stay at the Waldorf Astoria in New York for two years, and then let them come back with the amenities of Cadillacs, air conditioners, and beautiful juicy steaks at their table every day. Then when they come back, let them make the choice whether they want to live in the style of New Yorkers or as natural Penan in the tropical rain forest.

LIM KENG YAIK
Malaysian Minister of
Primary Commodities
interviewed in the
documentary film
*Can Tropical Rain
Forests Be Saved?*

Since the time of the British, successive governments in Sarawak have sought to draw the Penan out of the forest, encouraging them to settle along the major rivers, initially to facilitate trade and more recently to exert political control. Relocation invariably places the Penan in direct conflict with the riverine Dayaks, the Kayan and Kenyah peoples, in particular, who understandably resent the intrusion into what they regard as their traditional territory. The Penan are placed in a quandary. In order to claim their customary and legal rights as a Dayak people under Sarawak law they must act in a manner that compromises their tradition and inevitably antagonizes their neighbors. ❧

I was born in the forest. When I was still a child the government told us that if we settled we would have better lives, we would have schools and better facilities. That is how they induced us to settle. But my parents were not used to a settled life. They were afraid of the river, afraid of the heat. That's why they did not want to settle. At first they didn't accept; but the government continued to try to persuade them to settle. Again and again they tried to push us into settling. So finally our parents gave in and brought us down to the riverside.

UNYANG WAN
Long Iman
May 1993

opposite:
Long Bangan.

Unyang Wan and her husband, Tu'o Pejuman, in the government longhouse at Long Iman.

IAN MACKENZIE

The government persuaded us to settle on the riverside by promising us facilities, such as schools and clinics. We were summoned by the authorities to come to live on the riverside about thirty years ago.

There is no comparison between our present life and life in the forest. When I go to sleep, I don't have a good feeling, my stomach is empty. I'm hungry. My children are also hungry. You just listen to them crying all night, and when you see them, they are hungry. You can't compare this to life in the forest. Life was good before because you went to sleep with a full stomach. Then when I went to hunt, it was easy to find animals. You could go hunting at seven in the morning and come back at eight with a barking deer or a *babui*. Today you can't even find a squirrel. Even in a whole two weeks I wouldn't find the hair of one fleeing barking deer.

TU'O PEJUMAN
headman,
Long Iman
May 1993

A theme park near the capital city of Kuching, where Iban actors dress as Penan. At the Penan pavilion, a sign offers tourists the opportunity to "be taught how to use a blowpipe by an expert. Our Penan warrior will tell you how. Three darts for $1.00."

For any nomadic people, settlement implies the sacrifice of culture. The core of the relocation effort is an explicit attempt to absorb the Penan and all Dayak peoples into Malaysian society. Whether this should occur and just what it entails are not at issue. The only question raised by government planners is how soon this amorphous goal may be achieved. In a speech given at the opening of a theme park designed to display Sarawak's cultural diversity and constructed adjacent to the Holiday Inn Damai Beach resort, Chief Minister Taib Mahmud stated, "There is a big sociological question as to how fast they [the Penan] can be brought into the mainstream of development. But our answer is that there is nothing better than trying." Minister of the Environment and Tourism James Wong has reiterated the government position. "We don't want them running around like animals," he has said of the Penan. "The problem is to settle them down. They have to settle down, otherwise they have no rights." Clearly, nomadic rain forest dwellers do not fit the Malaysian image of a modern, developing nation.

Over the last several years the government has responded to the concerns of the Penan by proposing a series of initatives designed to facilitate assimilation. At great expense, and in part as a public relations gesture, a model longhouse was con-

Inside the longhouse at Batu Bungan.

IAN MACKENZIE

structed at Batu Bungan, a settlement adjacent to Gunung Mulu National Park. Similar facilities have been promised for other Penan communities. Other proposals promise to extend medical, educational, and technical services, including agricultural training designed to teach the use of tools, planting and clearing techniques, soil preparation, and even recipes for cooking forest foods. To date, however, few of these government programs have reached the Penan settlements. Given that, according to the government's own figures, over 20 percent of the residents of the national capital of Kuala Lumpur live as squatters, one might question whether the government is ultimately capable of delivering on its promise of socioeconomic development. A study conducted by the Flying Doctor Service in the hinterland of Sarawak reported that nearly a third of infants, almost half of toddlers, and three-quarters of preschool-aged children suffer from malnutrition. ❦

Father and son at Batu Bungan.

THOM HENLEY

NOMADS OF THE DAWN

The longhouse building is good, but that doesn't help you sleep well. I cannot go to sleep because I am hungry. If you want to give food to guests, you don't have money to buy it. You want to get animals in the forest like in the old days, and you can't get them. How are you going to feed your guests in this settlement? It's not like in the forest, where you can give them plenty of food. In the forest, you can give them as much as you want. Now, in the settlement, you just sit and stare at your guests, and you can't offer them anything.

TU'O PEJUMAN
headman
Long Iman
May 1993

 The longhouse is well built, out of boards, and it's painted, and we have mattresses, and we have pillows. But although we have mattresses and pillows there, we don't sleep well. Because every night, before we go to sleep, we think about what we need to eat, and what we are going to do the following day. These are the questions that are always in our hearts. That's why we can't sleep well, because we are thinking of what we are going to eat, and how we are going to find meat to feed our wives and our children. Because we can't eat our mattresses, and we can't eat our pillows. *Long Iman.*

MUTANG TU'O
Long Iman
May 1993

I was born in the forest, and it was an easy life as long as I stayed there. I just ate forest foods. I did not plant gardens. But now that I live in the longhouse, I do not have enough to eat. We plant things like this, but then we have to wait for weeks, and sometimes we harvest nothing, because there are many insects that eat our plants. That is why life in the longhouse is difficult, and it is hard to feed ourselves.

JULAN DÉNG
Interviewed in her
garden
Long Iman
May 1993

 Often the government says, "You should live here, here you will be happy, here is the best place for you." But in the place that they want us to live the sago is gone, and the trees have been destroyed, and all the land is ruined. Where could the children, where could the women go looking for rattan, go looking for sago, go looking for a place where there is food, if they ordered us to live in a place that has been ruined? Where could we find food? Where could we make a living? There is none. The animals are gone, the rivers are muddy. The animals are dead, because the trees have been destroyed, the land has eroded.

ASIK NYELIT
a nomad
Baa' Bila
April 1993

 And if we had to be in a place that is hot, like down there at the longhouse, our life would be difficult, we would feel like dying because there are no trees there, because there are no green leaves, everything is ruined, everywhere it's hot. That is the misfortune that one must endure at the longhouse.

LEJENG KUSIN
a nomad
Ubong River
May 1993

Long Iman.

Wherever there is the dirty smell of bare earth, or the smell of excrement and urine, there are mosquitoes. When the children go to take a bath, the water is dirty, and they will also be attacked by the mosquitoes. That is why people are always sick today. Nowadays, when people are sick, and they come to me, what medicine can I offer them? Before, if people came to you, you could just get medicine in the forest, and in two or three days they would be healed. This is one of the bad things about staying in the longhouse. You can't get medicine easily.

TU'O PEJUMAN
headman,
Long Iman
May 1993

One of the more tragic consequences of the relocation of the nomadic Penan has been the marked increase in the incidence and seriousness of certain diseases. When nomads, long accustomed to moving through the forest in small groups, become confined in large settlements, living together in squalid longhouses lacking any semblance of proper sanitation or potable water, the result is predictable. Over the last decade there has been a dramatic increase in morbidity due, in particular, to parasitic infections, dysentery, tuberculosis, conjunctivitis, and rheumatic fever. Fungal and staphylococcal infections are rampant. With incomplete immunization of children, diseases such as measles, mumps, rubella, and diphtheria are not uncommon. In many settlements, virtually every child is severely afflicted with head lice and scabies. Such skin conditions, though present in nomadic encampments, are far more serious and widespread in crowded longhouse communities.

Susceptibility to all forms of disease is increased due to the poor nutritional state of those living in the settlements. One child in two suffers some form of malnutrition, and deficiency in Vitamin A, in particular, has led to cases of keratomalacia, an eye disorder unknown in populations of nomadic Penan. Given these conditions, it is ironic that the government has promoted the prospect of improved health care as the rationale for relocation and settlement. In truth, the promised clinics seldom materialize, and those Penan living in longhouses must travel several days to receive even the most rudimentary medical care. A fly-in doctor service, much touted by the Sarawak government, is seriously deficient. Weather and funding permitting, isolated settlements are visited once a month, but in the hour allocated to each community, the physician is able to do little more than dispense painkillers such as Panadol. Thus, cut off from the forest that once supplied hundreds of medicinal plants, and inadequately serviced by the medical authorities of the state, the settled Penan find themselves caught in a vicious cycle of malnutrition and disease unlike anything known to their ancestors. ❦

I want to explain our custom in the forest. When we get a wild pig or a *nyakit* we will divide it equally among us; if it is little, the shares will be small; if it is big, we all get a big portion. Those people in the longhouse, when they get a wild pig, they just take it and eat it themselves. For us, in the forest, if we get a squirrel or a bird, even if it is small, we will share it equally. This is our traditional way, since the time of our ancestors. This is the way we live. And as for a bird or some other small animal, if it should be too small to be shared among all of us, we just give it to the children.

As for all the Penan who are in the settlements now, if you don't give money, they don't want to share. For example, if I were in a settlement, and I got a *babui*, if people didn't buy it from me, they wouldn't be able to eat. For us Penan in the forest, that is not our way. We in the forest, if we get *babui*, we share it equally. Even if it is fruit, we will divide it equally, even things that we get from downriver, even sugar and salt, we share that, too. But that is not so in the settlements. They take these things and eat them in their own dwelling. Big things, small things, anything they get, they just eat them in their own house, they don't share them. But as for us in the forest, it's not like that, we eat without using money, we eat enough, and we eat well. We don't depend on buying and selling.

Those who are settled in the longhouses built by the government, built by the logging companies, they don't live a good life. But we in the forest live a contented life, because we share. Even if they give us money, we divide it equally among all of us. This is the law of all us Penan who live in the forest.

We live without making a settlement. Even though we do not build houses, and make settlements, our lives are much better than those who do so. Those who are settled, like the Kayan, Kenyah, Kelabit, Chinese, and Malays do not live a good life because they depend on buying. And that is also the way of the Penan who are settled. It's foolish. It makes for a difficult life and bad customs, and even leads them to fight. But we in the forest, we have good relations with each other, we live with joy, and laughter, and happiness. Our life is complete. This is the life of the Penan who still live in the forest. As for those in the settlements, their customs are not good and not upright. This is the difference between life in the forest and life in the longhouse.

RÉMEN PAREN
Ubong River
May 1993

No one has the ethical right to deprive the Penan of the right to assimilation into Malaysian society.

JAMES WONG
Sarawak State Minister of the Environment and Tourism

Long Sabai, upper Tutoh River.

WADE DAVIS

NOMADS OF THE DAWN

We don't intend to turn the Penan into human zoological specimens, to be gawked at by tourists and studied by anthropologists while the rest of the world passes them by. . . . It's our policy to eventually bring all jungle dwellers into the mainstream. There is nothing romantic about these helpless, half-starved, and disease-ridden people.

MAHATHIR MOHAMAD
Prime Minister of Malaysia
To a meeting of European Community ministers
February 17, 1990

Big deal! The Europeans in England are saying that this woman is being deprived of a decent livelihood. I mean, she talks about children going to shoot monkeys. We're talking about children using computers. . . . People still shooting monkeys. Big deal! Some people actually believe this is the way these people should live. No schools, no nothing. Let them go walking around in a loincloth. . . . We have this [fascination for] exotic tribal life. Therefore don't touch this, and don't touch their cultural heritage, their burial grounds, and so on. And therefore stop logging. That is sick.

RAFIDAH AZIZ
Malaysian Minister of International Trade and Industry
commenting on a documentary film
May 1992

Implicit in the rhetoric and actions of the government is the assumption that the Penan are inherently incapable of choosing their own destiny, and that as primitive nomads long isolated in the jungle, they have simply missed the train of history. Viewed in this light the government has not only the right but the ethical obligation to help them catch up so that they, too, may benefit from the products and services of the modern age.

In truth, the Penan long ago made a choice, adopting the nomadic life-style they have consciously maintained over the centuries. Belying popular notions of progress, linguistic evidence strongly suggests that the ancestors of the Penan migrated to Borneo as farmers and only later abandoned agriculture to become hunters and gatherers. For any number of adaptive reasons, not the least of which may have been the ease of securing wild food, these people deliberately embraced the life of the nomad.

The history of the Penan defies yet another common assumption: the idea that a people remain nomadic and faithful to a rudimentary material culture only as long as they are cut off from the outside world. The Penan, in fact, have never been truly isolated from their neighbors. Nor have they rejected all outside influence. They have, in fact, displayed remarkable flexibility, adopting many innovations from surrounding cultures without compromising the integrity and essence of their own way of life. Throughout history, societies that have survived are those that have been fluid enough to adjust to new conditions, new possibilities, and new dreams.

The dexterity and ease with which the Penan convert raw steel into exquisite blades is a potent symbol of the culture's ability to incorporate on its own terms elements of the outside world. Obtaining steel bars through trade, the Penan construct simple but effective forges with bellows made of bamboo tubes, and a clever pumping mechanism that directs blasts of air across burning coals, readily generating temperatures that allow for the reworking of steel. Hammering red-hot steel into finely formed blades, the Penan create *parang* noted for their excellence and eagerly sought by neighboring groups. Like the machete, a *parang* is the basic tool used for harvesting, gathering firewood, clearing brush, and building shelters.

During the era of the White Rajahs, the Penan maintained constant contact with both the government and their Dayak neighbors through a supervised system of exchange known as *tamu*. Once every two or three months, temporary trading posts were established in the hinterland, often at the confluence of major rivers. At these open-air markets, the Penan acquired a variety of items including cloth, metal, salt, tobacco, firearms, ammunition, and cooking pots in exchange for their fine rattan mats and baskets, and their harvest of hornbill ivory, camphor, *damar, bezoar* stones, and fragrant medicinal woods such as *gaharu*. Under *tamu*, government officials regulated the trade and guaranteed fair prices for the Penan goods.

With a precise notion of time, but no traditional method of keeping track of months or years, the nomadic Penan mea-

A Penan forge.

sured the intervals between *tamu* by a simple system of knots tied in rattan. Each knot corresponded to a day and with every passing night one more would be untied. This mnemonic device, known as *tebukeu*, allowed the Penan consistently to appear on the appointed date, and thus ensured the integrity of the ritual trading exchange. Following independence and the departure of the British, the Sarawak government unilaterally broke the *tamu*. The last gathering on the Tutoh occurred in August 1966. A decade later the final exchange took place in the Ulu Baram. With the end of *tamu*, the Penan lost both their traditional access to equitable trade and their main line of communication with the government. As a result there is today no regular channel for the Penan to register their grievances and give testimony to their plight. ❧

Crossing the Melinau River at the end of a long journey.

RESISTANCE AND TRAGEDY

In 1987, Dayak resentment and anger over the impact of logging reached a flash point in the Baram and Limbang Districts. After having appealed in vain for over seven years to the government to put an end to the destruction of their traditional homelands, the Penan issued on February 13, 1987, a firm and eloquent declaration of their intentions:

"We, the Penan people of the Tutoh, Limbang, and Patah Rivers regions, declare: Stop destroying the forest or we will be forced to protect it. The forest is our livelihood. We have lived here since before any of you outsiders came. We fished in clean rivers and hunted in the jungle. We made our sago meat and ate the fruit of the trees. Our life was not easy but we lived it contentedly. Now the logging companies turn rivers to muddy streams and the jungle into devastation. Fish cannot survive in dirty rivers and wild animals will not live in devastated forest. You took advantage of our trusting nature and cheated us into unfair deals. By your doings you take away our livelihood and threaten our very lives. You make our people discontent. We want our ancestral land, the land we live off, back. We can use it in a wiser way. When you come to us, come as guests with respect.

"We, the representatives of the Penan people, urge you: Stop the destruction now. Stop all logging activities in the Limbang, Tutoh, and Patah. Give back to us what is properly ours. Save our lives, have respect for our culture. If you decide not to heed our request, we will protect our livelihood. We are a peace-loving people, but when our very lives are in danger, we will fight back. This is our message."

When this proclamation, like all the scores of letters, appeals, and petitions sent by Dayak peoples to state and regional authorities, was ignored, the Penan took direct action. On March 31, 1987, armed with their blowpipes, they erected the first of a series of blockades across a logging road in the Tutoh River basin. In April, one hundred Kayan at Uma Bawang blockaded a road that pierced their territory. In every instance, the actual barriers were flimsy, a few forest saplings bound with rattan. Their strength lay in the people that stood behind them. These human barricades, made up of men, women, and children, the old and the young, began as a quixotic gesture, a mere embarrassment to the government, but soon grew to a potent symbol of courage and resolve. Within eight weeks of the initial blockade, operations in sixteen logging camps had been brought to a halt, at a cost to the timber industry of several million dollars.

Resistance to the logging spread. By October 1987, Penan, Kayan, and Kelabit communities had shut down roads at

EVELYNE HONG

Penan resistance at Ulu Limbang.

twenty-three different sites in the Baram and Limbang Districts. In all, some 2,500 Penan from twenty-six settlements took part in the protest. For eight months, despite considerable hardship—hunger, heat exhaustion, and harassment by the logging interests—the indigenous peoples maintained their defiant, yet peaceful, blockades, disrupting the logging industry and frustrating state and federal authorities. The dramatic action electrified the environmental movement both in Malaysia and abroad, and drew worldwide support.

On the barricade.

Press coverage in Australia, Europe, and the United States stimulated concern that grew steadily into a sustained international campaign of protest. The Malaysian and Sarawak governments responded defensively, imposing severe restrictions on the media. Military and security forces were brought into play, and police joined the logging companies to assist in the dismantling of the blockades.

In October 1987, Malaysian Prime Minister Mahathir Mohamad, citing a wave of ethnic unrest threatening political instability, invoked the Internal Security Act of 1960 to incarcerate and suspend the rights of ninety-one critics of his regime. Among those detained was Harrison Ngau of Sahabat Alam (Friends of the Earth) Malaysia, a Kayan environmentalist and the most vocal supporter of the Dayak resistance. At the same time, forty-two Kayan natives of the village of Uma Bawang were arrested. Charged on three counts under the penal code, they were accused of obstructing the police, wrongful restraint, and unlawful occupation of state lands. The last charge, in particular, was received bitterly by the people of Uma Bawang, since they had established a blockade on their own land to protect their legally recognized customary rights.

The dramatic police action temporarily put an end to the blockades, but it precipitated a legal battle that exposed both an inherent contradiction in the government's position and the essential illegality of the logging itself. According to the Sarawak Land Code, native customary rights are inviolable. Since logging concessions had been granted by the state authorities without a clear demarcation of customary lands, the land rights of thousands of Dayak peoples had, by definition, been compromised and would continue to be violated as logging continued. On July 26, 1987, a Kayan charged with obstructing a public thoroughfare was acquitted when the magistrate concluded that the man had blocked a road that was part of customary land and thus had acted in a legitimate and legal defense of his customary rights.

To deflect the entire issue of customary rights, and to protect the logging industry, the state government took legislative action. In November 1987, it added to the Forest Ordinance amendment S90B, a specific provision that made it an offense for any person to obstruct the flow of traffic along any logging road. The law also permitted forestry officials to enlist the assistance of the agents of the logging concessionaire in the dismantling of any barrier or human obstruction. Penalties for violating amendment S90B were set at two years imprisonment and a fine of over U.S. $2,000.

With this deterrent in place, the government believed that the blockades would never again disrupt the flow of timber. They were wrong. The injustice of amendment S90B was obvious. 🌿

We who have rights to the land were, instead, arrested and not the timber companies who have caused damages to our land and properties. The law protects only the companies and causes us to suffer more. The law is not good. It unjustly allows outsiders and the logging companies to come and damage our land.

LOLÉÉ MIRAI
headman,
Long Léng
May 1988

In May 1988, the blockades went up again near Long Napir, bringing to a halt the logging operations of James Wong, Minister of the Environment and Tourism. Two more blockades sprang up in the upper Baram in September, and four more in October, as the indigenous peoples of the upper Limbang and Lawas areas joined the protest. Between November 1988 and January 1989, blockades occurred at seven sites, and the Sarawak Forestry Department arrested 128 Dayaks, mostly Penan. Many were held for a fortnight and then released. Some, unable to raise bail, were detained for a month.

By the middle of 1989, it appeared as if the government legislation, the repeated arrests, and the long and expensive trials had broken the resistance of the Dayak peoples. After January 1989, sporadic blockades, mounted by the Iban in Bintulu and the Penan in Baram, were quickly dismantled by the government. By July, the rate of logging in Sarawak had increased to over 700,000 acres a year, and in the Baram, timber operations were being carried out in three shifts, twenty-four hours a day. Then, on September 10, 1989, in a massive show of opposition, indigenous peoples in nineteen communities in the Upper Limbang and Baram erected twelve new barricades. Five days later, the action spread south into the Belaga area. On October 5, eleven Iban longhouse communities blockaded roads in the Bintulu District. By the end of the fall of 1989, an estimated four thousand Dayaks had joined the protest, successfully shutting down logging in nearly half of Sarawak. ❧

 The killers and the gangsters who work for the companies, they come and attack us. What can we do when the evil people come and do us harm? . . . If we are the victims of some incident, we are not numerous. If they should want to kill us, there are not many of us. And what could we do to stop them? That is what we are always thinking about. . . . We are always afraid of the gangsters who could attack at any moment. That is what we fear. And we are afraid of the cheaters and the liars who follow the company. It is hard for us because we are near the logging road, and we are afraid of people who might come, evil people who might rob us or kill us. That is what we are afraid of because we cannot run away, we cannot move, because we have an old man among us whose knees don't work. Whether good people or evil people want to find us, that is where we stay, from there we cannot move.

LEJENG KUSIN
Ubong River
May 1993

W ith pressure mounting, logging companies took the law into their own hands. Importing Chinese vigilantes from the city of Sibu, agents of the industry attempted to intimidate the indigenous peoples. Identity cards were confiscated, blowpipes and dart quivers thrown into rivers, individuals threatened and, in certain instances, physically beaten. A Japanese manager for a lumber company told the Penan at Long Napir: "If you don't have any food we'll provide it. But if you want compensation, I'll take your heads back to Japan. You have no right to demand anything in regard to the forest. From here to Batu Lawi, all the land is mine."

Sarawak officials did nothing to protect the indigenous peoples from harassment. On the contrary, in the wake of further protests, the government arrested another 117 Dayaks and subjected them to further human rights abuses. Hands bound behind their backs for the river journey to Miri from the upper Baram, Penan were compelled to urinate and defecate on themselves, all the while being ridiculed as animals by their guards. Once in Miri, eighty-six Penan men were held for two months in Lambir Prison, with inadequate food and water, in overcrowded cells infested with mosquitoes. Several had to be evacuated to the local hospital. In addition to physical deprivation, all suffered psychological trauma, not only due to their confinement but also because they knew that in their absence their families would be without food. Finally, on November 20, 1989, following an appeal to the chief justice, they were released. It had been the largest number of arrests to date and

the longest period of incarceration. The government appeared determined to break the spirit of the Dayak resistance with increasingly harsh and punitive measures. ❧

A pile of rejected logs left to rot by the roadside.

 In jail there are five to a cell, five feet square. They give us food, place it on the floor in front of us, and walk in it. In our culture this is very rude. Many have been sick. They would handcuff us, often one hand lashed to our ankles.

UNGA PAREN
headman, Long Bangan
Quoted in *Environment Guardian*
United Kingdom
November 2, 1990

On June 12, 1991, in yet another effort to establish a dialogue with the Sarawak government, over three hundred Penan erected a blockade near the village of Long Ajeng on a road leading into three of Sarawak's last uncut watersheds. As word of the blockade spread, hundreds of men, women, and children arrived from all parts of their territory. The logging companies responded aggressively. Food shipments destined for Long Ajeng were intercepted. In August a Penan man and woman were beaten to death by vigilantes. Nevertheless, in early 1992, there were still hundreds of Penan encamped at the barricade.

Finally, after eight months, authorities offered to meet with the Penan and promised at last to issue identity cards acknowledging their citizenship and allowing them the right to vote. In exchange, the Penan were to return to their villages. Faced with hunger, many Penan complied. One hundred refused, and soon were confronted by over a thousand fully armed riot police. ❦

The blockade near Long Ajeng, July 1991. The photo was taken during the seventh week of the blockade, soon after the Penan had successfully stood their ground against several dozen military police. The blockade was maintained for another seven months before being dismantled by an overwhelming force of armed riot police.

When the police came, they were in full gear with weapons, helmets, tear gas, and shields to protect their bodies. We had to leave because we were concerned for the women and children. If we had continued to stay at the blockade, we would have been killed.

Statement issued by Penan leaders Long Ajeng blockade March 14, 1992

On March 23, 1993, the Penan of the upper Baram initiated a third massive effort to halt the destruction of their ancestral homeland. People from twenty-one longhouses, a total of well over a thousand men, women, and children, erected a peaceful blockade at Long Mobui on the upper Sela'an, a tributary of the Baram River. Five days later twenty paramilitary personnel arrived and forcefully dismantled the wooden barrier. An hour later the Penan erected a new barrier. Several days later fifty fully armed soldiers and police officers appeared. The arrival of a thousand more was threatened. The Penan refused to move. Within the next three months, nine died of sickness and hunger, including two elders and six children.

Throughout the summer the standoff continued. Finally, on September 28, 1993, a force of three hundred soldiers, police, forestry officials, and employees of the logging company arrived in a caravan of forty-five vehicles. Under a veil of tear gas, on foot and in bulldozers, they attacked. ❦

All our huts were torn down with chain saws and burned. When we were disabled by the tear gas, the police and soldiers went on to destroy our barricade, which we had been guarding for nine months. The police had shields and helmets, and they were hitting us without any pity. Some of us bled and fell unconscious. All of our pet monkeys, hens, and dogs were killed. One very sick child died later [Sonny La'ot from Baa' Repo, six years old].

Penan statement
issued at Baa' Sebatu
October 22, 1993

The Penan consider the world beyond their forests to be an ominous and dangerous place. The mouths of their rivers are the edge of the sky, and the countries that lie beyond the sea are lands where people mingle freely with spirits. Despite these traditional beliefs, the Penan have chosen to join with other Dayaks to carry the message of their struggle to the entire world.

The campaign began with the defiance of the Dayak peoples, whose actions on the barricades captivated the international environmental community. The Dayak cause was taken up in Malaysia by Sahabat Alam Malaysia (SAM)—the national affiliate of Friends of the Earth. For several years, members of SAM, led by S. M. Mohd Idris, and represented in Sarawak by Harrison Ngau, had championed indigenous rights and rain forest preservation, and called for a moratorium on all logging activities in Sarawak. In 1987, Harrison Ngau was arrested and detained under the Internal Security Act. This flagrant abuse of justice drew international attention, not only to the victim but to the cause he championed.

In 1988, international concern became manifest in a series of dramatic developments. In July of that year, a motion was placed before the European Parliament calling for all member nations to ban timber imports from Sarawak until it could be demonstrated that the industry was not detrimental to the biological and cultural integrity of the region. The import ban did not pass, but it came close enough to stun Malaysian officials. In Australia, meanwhile, dock workers threatened to refuse to

unload timber imported from Malaysia. In Japan, Japan Tropical Forest Action Network (JATAN) called for a boycott of all tropical hardwoods, a strategy that was later taken up in the United States and Australia by the Rainforest Action Network. In Britain, several large furniture makers announced that they would no longer use certain tropical woods. In The Netherlands, municipal councils refused to grant building permits to construction projects that specified the use of tropical timber. In November 1989, a second motion came before the European Parliament calling for the release of all detainees in Sarawak, and the resolution of the conflict in a manner satisfactory to the indigenous peoples. This time the motion passed unanimously.

In 1990, support for the protection of the Sarawak forests grew, as media attention prompted spontaneous action by concerned individuals and organizations throughout the world. In September, two Penan representatives, Mutang Tu'o and Unga Paren, accompanied by Kelabit activist Anderson Mutang Urud, embarked on a world tour that took them to twenty-five cities in thirteen countries on four continents. In six weeks they spoke directly to an estimated fifty thousand people, and millions more saw them on television. Private meetings were held with a number of influential individuals, including U.S. Senator Al Gore; H.R.H. Prince Bernhard of The Netherlands; Madame Mitterand, First Lady of France; John Fraser, Speaker of Canada's House of Commons; and Maurice Strong, Secretary General of the UN Conference on Environment and

Development [the Earth Summit].

Lobbying efforts continued in the following year. In February 1991, Anderson Mutang Urud and Unga Paren traveled to Brussels to address a group of European parliamentarians. In July, Mutang spoke in Geneva to the United Nations Human Rights Commission and the UN Working Group on Indigenous People. Two months later, Mutang Tu'o and Mutang Urud traveled to New York and met privately with Javier Perez de Cuellar, then Secretary General of the United Nations. In January 1992, Svend Robinson, Canadian member of Parliament, went to Sarawak as part of a human rights mission to Asia. Against the wishes of the Malaysian government, and guided by Mutang, he traveled to the Long Ajeng blockade, and later issued a strong condemnation of the Sarawak government.

On February 5, 1992, three weeks before the dismantling of the Long Ajeng blockade, Anderson Mutang Urud was arrested without charge, held in a windowless room, denied adequate clothing or drinking water, threatened with violence, and interrogated around the clock. On March 4, he was formally charged with operating an illegal society, the Sarawak Indigenous Peoples Association, and released on bail, with a trial set for September. He was warned of dire consequences if he engaged in further international campaigning. Advised by his lawyers that he faced certain incarceration under the Internal Security Act, he left the country in March and entered exile in Canada.

Mutang's case became an issue of international concern.

THOM HENLEY

During a world tour to gain support for their struggle, Anderson Mutang Urud and Unga Paren light candles in Notre Dame Cathedral, Paris.

His treatment by the Sarawak authorities was condemned universally in the Western media and by politicians, church leaders, and the environmental community. On April 2, in Washington, U.S. Senator Al Gore introduced Senate Resolution 280, which called for the protection of the Sarawak rain forest and the rights of all indigenous peoples in the state. In May 1992, Mutang Urud brought the campaign to the Earth Summit in Rio de Janeiro. On December 10, representing all the Dayak peoples of Sarawak, Anderson Mutang Urud addressed the 47th Session of the General Assembly of the United Nations. ❧

[The anti-logging protests are] being used to set up an international infrastructure that can attack and topple the sovereign governments of third world nations, using the excuse of saving the environment.

MAHATHIR MOHAMAD
Prime Minister of Malaysia
Quoted in
The Economist
February 15, 1992

 The government says that it is bringing us progress and development. But the only development that we see is dusty logging roads and relocation camps. For us, their so-called progress means only starvation, dependence, helplessness, the destruction of our culture, and the demoralization of our people. The government says it is creating jobs for our people. But these jobs will disappear along with the forest. In ten years, the jobs will all be gone, and the forest which has sustained us for thousands of years will be gone with them.

Why do we need jobs? My father and my grandfather did not have to ask the government for jobs. They were never unemployed. They lived from the land and from the forest. It was a good life. We had much leisure time, yet we were never hungry, or in need. These company jobs take men away from their families for months at a time. They are breaking apart the vital links that have held our families and our communities together for generations. These jobs bring our people into a consumer economy for which they are not prepared.

An old man I know once asked a policeman why it was he could not blockade a road on his own land. The policeman told him that Yayasan Sarawak had been given the license to log the forest, and so the land belongs to the company. This is what the old man said in reply: "Who is this Yayasan Sarawak? If he really owns the land, why have I never met him in the forest during my hunting trips over the last sixty years?"

A woman I know who has seven children once came to me and said, "This logging is like a big tree that has fallen on my chest. I often awake in the middle of the night, and I and my husband talk endlessly about the future of our children. I always ask myself, when will it end?"

ANDERSON MUTANG URUD
Address to the UN General Assembly
December 10, 1992

THOM HENLEY

... You are where we keep our hearts, and we rely upon you. To wherever you return, to whatever country, until you reach your own house and your own family, until you reach your minister or your king, I hope that everything that I have said, that I have communicated today, will not be lost, and I want you to pass on everything I have said to your people there. I hope that it will not be lost.

I am not speaking in jest, I am not inventing stories. I am speaking with great sincerity. I am not saying that things here are good, I am not saying that the situation here is happy. On the contrary, I am telling you all the problems. There is no happiness now.

That is what I am telling you. It is truly difficult, it is hard for me to hunt animals here. You, yourself, with the eyes in your own head, you have seen the land around here. You have seen the land that has been laid waste, the trees that have been destroyed, you have seen the sago that has been uprooted, you have seen the *tajem* trees and the fruit trees that have been felled.

If your governments, or if you white people don't come and help us, surely it will be the end of life for us Penan. Our hardships are overwhelming us. I who say this, Wéé Salau, my fate is to live only another two or three years, and perhaps I will die in the coming year. If I die, there is no one else who can speak as I have spoken. Perhaps what I know will die with me. Perhaps when you come again in a year or two you will meet only these children; perhaps only these children will remain.

There is no other person as old as myself now. And there is no other old person who can tell you our story from former days up until the present. And we hope with hearts as big as this river, as big as that mountain, as big as the heavens, that you will be able to help us.

WÉÉ SALAU
the elder headman,
Ubong River band
Baa' Bila
April 1993

Wéé Salau died in 1994.